Encounter God and Engage

The Dynamic Connection Between Knowing and Being

RICHARD O'RILEY

Copyright 2026 by Richard O'Riley

All rights reserved, including the right to reproduce this book or portions thereof in any form whatsoever. For permission requests, write to the author at oriley6@aol.com.

Logo design by Andrew Hakes.

Produced by Inksnatcher.com.

Printed in the United States of America.

LCCN record available at https://lccn.loc.gov/Library of Congress Cataloging-in-Publication Data

Names: O'Riley, Richard, author

Title: Encounter God and Engage: The Dynamic Connection Between Knowing and Being Known / Richard O'Riley

Subjects: | BISAC: RELIGION/Christian Living/Inspirational | RELIGION/Christian Living/Spiritual Growth | RELIGION/Christian Ministry/Evangelism

Description: First edition. | Celtic Cottage Press, Rochester, NY, 2025. | Summary: "Blending biblical insight, personal testimony, and practical wisdom, this book shows how true spiritual encounters with God move us beyond moments of inspiration into a life of active engagement, faith, and transformation." —Provided by publisher.

Identifiers: LCCN 2025921812 | 978-1-7357980-7-3 (paperback) | 978-1-7357980-6-6 (hardback) | 978-1-7357980-8-0 (e-book)

Unless otherwise noted, all Scripture quotations are taken from the New King James Version® (NKJV). Copyright © 1982 by Thomas Nelson. Used by permission. All rights reserved.

Scripture quotations marked (AMP) are Scripture quotations taken from the Amplified® Bible (AMP), Copyright © 2015 by The Lockman Foundation. Used by permission. lockman.org

Scripture quotations marked (KJV) are from the King James Version of the Bible, which is in the public domain in the United States.

Scripture quotations marked (NIV) are taken from The Holy Bible, New International Version®, NIV®. Copyright © 1973, 1978, 1984, 2011 by Biblica, Inc. Used with permission of Zondervan. All rights reserved worldwide. www.zondervan.com

For information about special discounts for bulk purchases, please contact the author at oriley6@aol.com.

To all those who have chosen to learn not only what the Bible tells about God, but also to know the ways of God and to experience Him through active partnership. He is the God who has called us to join Him in advancing His kingdom according to the eternal plan He has chosen for us in Christ.

Table of Contents

Preface i

Introduction:
Encounter God and Engage: Dynamic Connection v

Part One: Open Disclosures... 1

   1. A Look Back 3
   2. Connections in the Discourse of Events 7
   3. Once Upon a Dream 11
   4. The Anchor of Our Souls 13
   5. The Operative Law of Faith in Action 19
   6. Behold and Become 23
   7. Choice, the Unescapable Imperative 27
   8. Call and Response 31
   9. Mirror, Mirror on the Wall................................... 35
   10. Hallways, Bridges, and Distant Doorways 39
   11. As You Go.. 43
   12. Cleanup Time 49
   13. Caught in the Middle... 51
   14. From Here to Eternity 55

Part Two: Biblical Accounts of the Encounter/
        Engagement Dynamic... 57

   15. The Courts of Heaven 59
   16. Hammered, Heated, and Honed 63

17. A Hospital of Hope or a Hospital of Despair 67

18. David, the First Rock Star 77

Part Three: Encounter/Engage, Personal Accounts 81

19. The Man in the Streets 83

20. Encounter Gone Bad 89

21. Innocent as Doves but Wise as Serpents 95

Part Four: Where in the World Are We? Current Status 97

22. Agents of Dynamic Change 99

23. Called to Bring Encounter 103

24. Jesus, Our Pattern and Path 105

25. Taking It to the Streets 111

26. Out of the Saltshaker 115

27. Onward Christian Soldiers 123

28. Heaven to Earth 125

29. Encounter: My Time Had Come 129

30. Close Encounters of the Third Kind 131

31. Jailbreak 135

32. Silver and Gold 139

33. Back on Your Feet, Out of the Shade
    and Into the Heat 145

34. I Heard It at the Drinking Fountain 149

35. Some Tools of the Trade 153

Part Five: Marching Orders 157

36. Discipling the Disciples 159
37. Gathering His Worshippers 163
38. Served or Serving? 165
39. Not All That Glitters Is Gold 169
40. When Encounter Brings Conflict 175
41. No One Is an Island 179
42. Ambassadors of the Word 181
43. Revived to Revive: A Bit of History 185
44. The Weaver and the Web that He Made 189
45. The Battle Belongs to the Lord 191
46. Last Call 199

About the Author 203

Preface

Shortly after a few COVID-19 restrictions on church gatherings were lifted in mid-2020, our church reopened for services. I observed how a strong revivalist appeal and powerful Sunday worship continually drew many. People could now sit in proximity during prayer, have limited altar calls, and begin to fellowship after services. Seeing the numbers pouring in was exciting, especially the new influx of young adults drawn by contemporary worship and strong preaching. I recall being a new convert during the Jesus Movement of the early 1970s and being again refreshed with the new enthusiasm and energy. At that time, we were fortunate to have had the benefit of good teaching and mentorship, which grounded us in the Word and proved invaluable. Those days are now long gone. However, I hope to rekindle that enthusiasm and re-establish some essential foundations for current and future generations. From those early days, our life challenges would prove our resolve and strengthen our faith as we held fast to our convictions and strong foundations.

This book is based on the insights I have acquired through years of observing, reflecting, questioning, and learning. Although I've always appreciated Sunday celebrations, it was the rest of the week, with its hills and valleys, where faith was tested and sustaining grace overcame many obstacles. It is no secret that taking one step at a time would eventually lead to the significant victories we have come to enjoy. Sometimes, the mundane aspects of daily life remind me of the exploits recorded in the book of Acts: Between the significant events, there must have been many Mondays.

I have always enjoyed times of praise and have been active in accompanying and leading worship for many years. There were times when a sense of God's presence was almost overwhelming. We were also taught that worship was the highest calling for all creation, and that all creation was waiting for the children of God to lead the way in a procession of praise. In the early years, we were also schooled in the Word and were taught the importance of walking in faith and overcoming. Maturity meant learning to hear the Spirit and walking in His counsel. As time passed, learning how to encourage and minister to others was a necessary part of Christian commitment and, of course, a divine privilege.

Some of my inspiration for this book is taken from Acts 14. After Paul and Barnabas completed their first missionary journey, they returned to the church at Jerusalem to settle the issue of circumcision. Along the way, they checked in on the cities where they had previously converted many and set up churches in Asia Minor. They traveled through Lystra, Iconium, and Antioch, "strengthening the souls of the disciples, exhorting them to continue in the faith and saying, 'We must through many tribulations enter the kingdom of God'" (Acts 14:21–22). From this verse, I've gained an understanding that one may be converted through an encounter with Jesus; however, initial salvation is a gateway, a starting point into a walk where we learn to engage and grow in our knowledge and maturity in Christ. We need the strengthening that worship, praise, and prayer bring, but encouragement, exhortation, and perseverance are also necessary components for growth and development. Otherwise, we continue as babes—desiring the milk of the Word and remain unskilled in ministry (Hebrews 5:12). I hope to enlighten the reader to see that from the safe harbor of encounter, we are ultimately meant to be equipped and deployed on a venture that can only happen through faith and partnership with the Captain of Our Salvation.

I don't mean to imply that devotional encounters cannot provide instant transformation. When we encounter the holy presence of our Lord in times of personal and corporate worship, our spirits are refreshed indeed. The Word says that "In His presence, there's fullness of joy, and at His right hand there's pleasure evermore" (Ps. 16:11). A key revelation struck me after writing this book. Encounter alone is a gateway to a relationship with God and His ultimate eternal purposes. Jesus did not come preaching an encounter but proclaimed the kingdom of God. Knowing that maturity can only be developed through obedience, we must, by design, pass through tests and the trials of our faith, transforming us from glory to glory. Therefore, godly character is not developed primarily in our weekly or daily devotional encounters, but rather through the trust, perseverance, and single-mindedness required in worldly encounters and personal relationships.

I believe it is our failure to act upon God's prompting; however, that has stymied and even crippled us from walking in a greater dimension of godly character and individual callings. I've included biblical examples of those who embraced their destinies and a few who refused their divine opportunity. No such account, however, would be complete without a few of my own testimonies regarding significant encounters and engagements, as you will see.

Much of what we have been given requires our acceptance; therefore, we must willingly receive what has been bestowed upon us. However, receiving is yet a prequel to engagement. What we do with what is freely given determines its value and purpose. Does the mere fact that each received the Master's endowment of eternal life complete God's ultimate intention for our lives? Consider Ecclesiastes 11:1, "Cast your bread upon the waters, For you will find it after many days," and, "He who observes the wind will not sow, And he who regards the clouds will not reap" (v. 4). In the following chapters, I will elaborate on understanding a godly encounter, its call, and our response toward apprehending and engaging in dynamic connections that direct us in fulfilling the high call we have in Christ.

Hopefully, the following pages will help answer the question posed by the children of Israel when confronted by the prophet Ezekiel, "How should we then live?" (Eze. 33:10). To demonstrate kingdom life, we must learn to walk like Jesus did on this earth—in trust and surrender. I intend to broaden our understanding of how God has made provision for us to embrace the precious times of encounter and partner with Him as He works in us to will and do His good pleasure.

INTRODUCTION

ENCOUNTER GOD AND ENGAGE: DYNAMIC CONNECTION

Today, many charismatic churches describe "spiritual encounter" as a devotional event that typically occurs during the worship portion of their weekly church service. It is a time when the saints focus on God's presence filling the sanctuary. Some would say it is a time when hearts acknowledge the Holy Spirit bearing witness to their spirits, when supernatural awe falls upon the congregation, lifting hearts and emotions, and bringing encouragement, edification, and comfort. By turning to Jesus, many have found relief from anxieties and concerns stemming from daily pressures and life's challenges. As many "soak in the moment," they often testify to a renewal of faith and restored hope.

It is a precious moment whereby we corporately engage with our eternal Creator as our spirits are refreshed and recharged. In a sermon, once upon a time, I recall a preacher proclaiming that all encounters with the Spirit of God are transformational and provide opportunities to both encounter and be renewed in His presence. That moment of divine connection draws the hearts of man and God into a sacred union. Heaven's account only measures the value and purpose of an encounter. However, it remains essential to understand that, as much as we may be drawn to and cherish the event, God ultimately initiates heavenly encounters.

What I have termed a devotional encounter, whether corporately or privately, is a unique and precious experience. Encounter with His Father was at the center of Jesus's heavenly relationship in eternity, and while He walked on earth. From the beginning, God created man in His image. However, both Adam and Eve were created innocent. According to the divine plan, their maturity would involve obedience, commission, and choice. The guidelines for such a glorious epic were made clear. However, through one man's disobedience and through deceit, a counterfeit encounter and engagement episode led to humanity's downfall. Even then, a plan for redemption, connection, and restoration was set into motion.

I distinguish between devotional encounters and what I describe as encounter/engagement events—where God shows up in the present to provide direction, encouragement, affirmation, instruction, wisdom, or warning, with a specific purpose in mind. In Romans 5:3–4, the apostle Paul speaks of a proven character developed through trials, problems, and suffering. Devotion is necessary, yet through perseverance and endurance, we inherit God's promises and Christ's character emerges, all producing hope.

Divine encounters are a recurring theme throughout numerous biblical accounts. It is the starting point for the events that shape and unfold God's eternal purpose for mankind. Scripture provides several examples of how a heaven-to-earth connection serves a divine purpose. For example, Jacob's vision at Bethel offers a graphic depiction of this exchange, as does the angelic intervention that prevents Isaac's sacrifice at Abraham's hand. We witness God's notable heavenly encounters with Abraham, Moses, Joseph, Gideon, David, Solomon, and the prophets throughout the Old Testament. In the New Testament, we learn that Saul, on the road to Damascus, and the apostle John, on the island of Patmos, experienced personal events that inaugurated Christianity. These accounts sum up the unfolding and greatest story ever told. We recognize heavenly hosts, such as Gabriel, who appeared to young Mary, who were appointed and initiated according to eternal purposes and divine timing.

Through the agency of the encounter and His engaging dynamic, God provides the means of expressing His intention to humanity while empowering them to carry out His eternal purposes on earth. In this latter case, encounter is both an invitation and a commission. Whether through miracles, angelic encounters, or the still small voice spoken to those willing to hear what the Spirit says, God establishes the lines of communication, and, through Christ, has granted us the ability to listen and discern His will. However, our willingness to embrace and engage in the Father's prompting releases His divine power, which enables us to fulfill His purposes. "Abraham believed God, and it was accounted to him for righteousness. ... He did not waver at the promise of God through unbelief, but was strengthened in faith, giving glory to God, [21] and being fully convinced that what He had promised He was also able to perform" (Rom. 4:3, 20–21).

In Romans 10, Paul declares that faith comes through hearing God's word (v. 17). God's word empowers the hearer through the written word (logos) and the internal witness of the Spirit (rhema), imparting faith and the ability to obey. In other words, agreeing with God's word empowers the hearer. It is a divine partnership that releases God to stretch forth His hand to confirm His Word with signs and wonders.

Ezekiel was given a heavenly overview of a desolate terrain. Upon this, he was asked to speak about what he had seen. He was then instructed to make specific declarations. God's power was now released in the earthly realm. That which had once lived had dissipated, but then, it was revived, became strong, and made ready to advance and do exploits (Ezek. 37:1–14). The dynamic connection within this pairing of encounter/engage is key for advancing God's heavenly invasion of the earth. As an army, we are overcomers, having been predestined to His campaigns.

I'm reminded of Romans 8:22–23, which speaks of the labor pains that all creation is currently experiencing in anticipation of the advancement of God's kingdom. This invasion, purposed since before the earth's foundation, will only be accomplished through the response of a warrior bride fully engaged in the call of God, especially in these uncertain and critical times.

While the 120 tarried in the upper room, the wind of the Holy Spirit blew in, filling the room and the faithful present. Following that fateful moment, Peter is found quoting the prophet Joel, declaring that the Spirit shall be poured out on all mankind (Acts 2:17–18). The future tense is used here; however, it may also be considered the future perfect tense, as we continuously experience the Holy Spirit at work within us, comforting, empowering, and guiding us into truth. The book of Acts, as written by Luke, most vividly portrays the acts of the Holy Spirit. From the Holy Spirit within us and upon us comes the resurrection power that worked in Christ and now works in us who call upon Him who rose from the dead.

And so, the church was born, empowered by believers who would take the good news to the nations, bearing witness through signs and wonders. With that, we mark the words of George Handel's "Messiah," which so eloquently proclaim, "The kingdoms of this world have become *the kingdoms* of our Lord and of His Christ, and He shall reign forever and ever!" (Rev.11:15). It is the Spirit that has never ceased laboring, along with the holy angels, to reveal the riches of His glory in the saints and bear witness to God's glory in all creation. And so, we define *encounter* as having God's continued intervention and abiding presence with us here in the earthly realm.

Throughout the two millennia of the New Testament, large-scale waves of heavenly visitations have been referred to as awakenings, revivals, times of refreshment, or simply significant moves of the Holy Spirit. Movements, however, are more accurately identified after the fact, as a historical account is rightly a post-occurring record. It is usually written following specifically identifiable times and events. Notwithstanding, as time passes, much becomes filtered through oral tradition, interpretation, or modern vernacular. Inherently, during such occurrences, perspective becomes vulnerable to change. Is it the best of times, the worst of times, or both? As with the title of Charles Dickens' immortal novel *A Tale of Two Cities*, we must wait until the tale is told and subject to the passage of time.

In the present day, a popular movement, now referred to as "Encounter," has risen among Western Christian churches, especially here in the USA. It is my aim, however, throughout the following narratives to distinguish between our devotional lives as lovers of the One who first loved us and calls us to rejoice in His presence with hearts and hands lifted, and walking out a life that demonstrates His directives for overcoming in this world and manifesting His goodness as He did on earth.

However, as we encounter the nature and heart of our God, we are compelled to boldly proclaim Him as we step into our callings as witnesses and soldiers for the cause of Christ. In these uncertain times, our roles as lovers and warriors are critical. However, as warriors and statesmen, we must discern the heavens descending upon us in manifest power and wisdom, hear the call as it applies to each of us, and respond.

While not ignoring tumultuous times and events, we are called to look up, lift our heads, for our redemption draws near (Luke 21:28). As a preacher once put it: Look up, for your redemption is coming to a theater near you. Alignment in the defining aspects of Christ's character is crucial to our overcoming and shining as lights in an increasingly darkening world. All too often, we tend to avoid controversial topics that face us outside the church, leaving public service, community affairs, and local politics up to those with secular interests and influence.

Without a broader vision of what Christ intends for His church, we lose perspective of God's purpose for our election. When this happens, we are left in a state where churches become selective, overemphasizing one aspect of spirituality to the exclusion of all others. Unfortunately, with little vision, we live with a tendency to live from sermon to sermon and church event to church event.

We need to return to where authentic encounter meets active engagement, where superficial distraction takes a back seat to kingdom-advancing priorities. I must reiterate that when it comes to times of worship and devotion, an encounter with God's presence transforms us, assuring us of eternal salvation and allowing us to witness His indwelling presence within our hearts and minds. The encounter experience I focus on throughout this narrative will primarily deal with walking out our faith in partnership with our Savior as He leads us from glory to glory.

In the following chapters, through various examples of the encounter/engage axiom, I will attempt to demonstrate how the human enterprise is enacted through God's initiative and our response. We will see the beauty of a loving God who has ordained these statutes and displays His kind intention and eternal destiny for us, His chosen. I've included thoughts from observations I've made over time, hoping to shed light on misconceptions, assumptions, and unbiblical interpretations that have led many to fall short of a proper understanding of faith and its practical application.

The connection between encounter and engagement yields a spiritual dynamic in us in ways we could never have imagined. Our encounter with Christ and the infilling of His Holy Spirit has brought us to a time when creation is waiting in anticipation for the children of God to rise, not only as a habitation of God but as an army that will walk out the exploits God has predestined for them. I hope that what follows in these pages will not only shed light on our greater calling in Christ but also empower us as a redemptive force willing to bring good news to society.

Part 1 of this book addresses definitions and biblical concepts relevant to the dynamic of encounter and engagement. Part 2 illustrates accounts within the Old and New Testaments where we look over the shoulders of individuals as they encounter and engage in events that transform them through God's intervention. In part 3, I have included some personal testimonials to encourage others. Part 4 explores additional applications of encounter and engagement dynamics. Part five provides incentives for us to carry out the Great Commission.

PART ONE

OPEN DISCLOSURES

CHAPTER 1

A Look Back

The Bible says, "In the beginning God created the heavens and the earth.... God saw everything that He had made, and indeed it was very good" (Gen. 1:1, 31). The first events in creation, told in Genesis, the book of beginnings, are where our comprehension of all that follows between the immovable mover and what springs into being from His command starts.

So, which dynamic occurred first: encounter or engage? My dear wife has always maintained a simple fact: "God is a verb." Although no chapter and verse explicitly state this, let's examine this active paradigm. God said, "Let there be light" (Gen. 1:3), and commanded the light to shine out of the darkness (Gen. 1:4). Does this not set all cause and effect into motion? There must first be a natural cause to the natural mind, followed by an effect. When starting with God, who is supernatural, there need not be a physical cause, only the manifestation of divine intent. We could compare this dilemma to just how Mary, the mother of Christ, was impregnated. Perhaps the entire question of the incarnation should be considered a mystery, and leave it at that.

God is light, and immediately upon His command and by His nature, both the spiritual and physical realms, along with time and space, sprang into existence. God initiated the boundaries of time and space to provide context for the physical universe and to contain the natural creation. Within the early void, there may have been only what astrophysicists call the *unified field theory*. The theory was first proposed by Albert Einstein following James Clerk Maxwell's earlier field theory of electromagnetism. The theory described a temporary condition in which all electromagnetic energy, gravity, and fundamental nuclear forces existed simultaneously. The early cosmos contained no subatomic particles, atoms, or any recognizable matter, such as solids, liquids, or gases.

As the physical laws of thermodynamics dictate, the universe expanded, and as it cooled, it allowed subatomic particles to form the chemical elements. The stars of heaven were born from the fusion of simple hydrogen atoms. This profusion of glowing matter, now shepherded by gravity, was drawn into billions of majestic galaxies that now declare the glory of God. Orbiting the stars, cooler matter condensed into worlds we know as planets. As God pondered the cosmos, His Spirit brooded over what had happened up to this point. The Spirit recognized only disarray and little evidence of the majesty attributable to God's creative intention and, therefore, the Spirit commenced the task of fashioning order and goodness out of the chaos.

Having completed the earth and all its fullness thereof, God rested. Encountering the virtue of His creation, God spoke again and called the fruit of His action good. According to the order of creation, it would appear that there was another call within God's heart. Seeing that it was not good for His Son to be uniquely alone, the Father desired a bride for His Son. They would be engaged in an eternal enterprise that began in a garden and would eventually culminate in a city, where the angelic hosts of heaven would celebrate the marriage of the Lamb. God's intention and creative act preceded His first encounter, spoken in the heavens with a resounding "It is good."

The two components of the encounter/engagement dynamic are inseparable and cyclical, having the ability to directly move each other in a contextual relationship together with an all-powerful and loving God.

In my sophomore year of college, during a Philosophy 101 lecture, my professor brought up the classical argument for verifying the existence of God. By way of deductive reasoning,

Greek philosophers, such as Aristotle, concluded that there must have been an "unmoved mover" outside of time that initiated existence within time. Implicit in the name, the "unmoved mover" is whatever or whomever moves all other things, while any prior action does not move the mover. Later, in the 13th century, Thomas Aquinas reintroduced this ancient concept in his argument for the existence of God. Aquinas concluded that nothing moves without a prior mover. This naturally leads to a regression of movers, which can only be resolved by identifying a first mover, God Himself. Therefore, the idea of an infinite past contradicts the modern cosmological theory that the universe originated from a spontaneous, catastrophic event called the "Big Bang." We're not speaking of a contemporary TV sitcom here, but of a monumental event, now estimated to have occurred some 13.7 billion years ago, during which everything supposedly emerged out of nothing.

God is light. It follows that light would reveal His creation. It's indisputable that we need to have visible light to observe an object. As we gaze up at a dark sky on a clear night, myriads of insipid points of light give testimony of an expanse beyond our comprehension. In one of the most poetic psalms, David writes, "The heavens declare the glory of God; And the firmament shows His handiwork" (Ps. 19:1).

As we establish a divine sequence that begins with engagement, we should include the nature of God Himself. A word that may assist us here is "exogenous"—originating from or caused by factors outside a system, organism, or process. We understand that God exists independent of His creation; His character and attributes are eternal and unchanging. God is love, and God is light. God did not need to encounter Himself, but gave expression to creation in the hope that we would be before Him, "holy and blameless in His sight" (Col. 1:22).

From the instant God said, "Let there be light," the Holy Spirit engaged creation through acts purposed by the Father, articulated by the Son, and carried out by the Spirit. Through the agency of the Holy Spirit, we are led to what initiates, motivates, and empowers us, according to the simple law of cause and effect. Jesus, the exact representation of the Father, was the light shining into the darkness. To as many as receive Him and believe, He gives power to become all He intends. Therefore, the two components of the encounter/engagement dynamic are inseparable and cyclical, having the ability to directly move each other in a contextual relationship with an all-powerful and loving God.

From a biblical perspective, we can then understand when John says, "In this is love, not that we loved God, but that He loved us" (1 Jn. 4:10). The Bible is consistently repetitive with this theme throughout, i.e., where God initiates divine encounters, whether in our devotion or the call to action. It only follows that all creation follows in the manifold wisdom of His order and governance, which forever rides upon His shoulder. In contrast, for us, His sheep, He reserves both shoulders. "And when he finds it [the lost sheep], he joyfully puts it on his shoulders and goes home" (Lk. 15:5–6 NIV, brackets and emphasis added).

CHAPTER 2

Connections in the Discourse of Events

Launched in 1948, the radio broadcast *Candid Microphone* was introduced to television in the 1950s on the American Broadcasting Company (ABC) as *Candid Camera*. It served as a precursor to modern-day reality TV. Each episode began with a person going about their daily routine before being unexpectedly thrown off their course by a predetermined event or personal encounter. People encountered items like talking mailboxes or saw their bowling balls return without finger holes. Most only realized they had been set up when they heard the show's tagline: "Smile, you're on Candid Camera." This intrusion, affecting subsequent actions and unrehearsed responses, was the entertainment factor as viewed by home audiences. This classic TV program serves as a light-hearted analogy that supports my theme of encounter and engagement.

As mentioned earlier, divine encounters are not exclusive to Sundays. As we go about our routines, duties, or daily activities, we often encounter momentary interruptions that require simple adjustments or quick decisions. However, notification of a family crisis or pending physical threats will immediately draw our more profound attention and response. I've seen that committing to long-term responsibilities requires deeper assessment, reflection, and prayer, leading to responsible outcomes. The TV show, although written for a secular audience, offers a brief glimpse into the dynamic of the encounter or engagement experience, where God meets us in the moment and waits for our response. Through His guidance and the exercise of our faith, we engage in a path of righteousness and walk from glory to glory.

Further illustrating the connections between events and the outcomes they set in motion, I refer to another long-running game show, Truth or Consequences. Contestants were asked a question that had little likelihood of being successfully answered. A stunt or humorous activity was assigned for failure. The entertainment value kept the audience laughing as they shared in watching the actions and reactions played out. These two examples illustrate the principle that for every action, there is a reaction.

In his first law of motion—commonly called the law of inertia—Isaac Newton states that an object at rest remains at rest unless acted upon by an external force. Once in motion, the object will continue in one direction at a constant speed unless acted upon by an outside force. It has been said that man did not invent natural law; he only discovered it and developed systems to observe, measure, and record his findings. Natural law reflects spiritual law. From this axiom, we know that Jesus is both the Creator and the One who holds all things together by the word of His power.

Moving then from natural law to spiritual law, we see that consequences follow actions, as in, "a man reaps what he sows" (Gal. 6:7 NIV). Two common Scriptures can be used to illustrate this point: "The wages of sin is death" (Rom. 6:23). Or, on a more positive note, "the law of the Spirit of life in Christ Jesus has made [us] free from the law of sin and death" (Rom. 8:2). Thankfully, we are no longer children of wrath, but through the death, burial, and resurrection of Christ from the dead we are raised to walk in newness of life continually. Hallelujah.

In many cases, a divine encounter is an invitation to a revelation of the Father's glory, heart, and fellowship. However, with encounter, it is often a call to come away with Him for a divine opportunity for the Holy Spirit to give us counsel, wisdom, and direction; with such also comes assurance and more profound revelation. Encounters can bring correction, conviction, admonition, and rebuke. How often do we consider these last interdictions as painful or dismissive of our regard or sensitivities?

The Father's chastening is always for our benefit. How frequently do we fail to embrace discipline as rungs on a ladder that allow us to rise, dismiss the unredeemed presumptions we rest upon, and walk at liberty as free saints?

Natural law reflects divine or supernatural law. To clarify, the law of sin and death here does not refer to the physical laws that govern matter, energy, and time. Instead, it pertains to the knowledge of good and evil. It represents a decision between two trees, imposed by the tree that stood in the garden of Eden as an alternative for walking in the light and fellowship with God.

Under the divine ordinance, whether under the law of Moses or that of the Spirit in the New Testament, we see a connection: sin results in death, while obedience results in righteousness. Each choice binds us to an outcome. "The disobedience of one man enslaved many to destruction, whereas by the obedience of one man, we were made righteous" (Rom. 5:19).

> *The Father's chastening is always for our benefit. How often do we fail to embrace discipline as rungs on a ladder that allow us to rise, dismiss the unredeemed presumptions we rest upon, and walk at liberty as free saints?*

Under the law operating in the Spirit of life, we have been set free to be married to another, even to Christ, that we may walk in the eternal purposes God intended for us. As He made provision for our justification, He also now makes it possible, by his ever-indwelling Spirit, to glorify us even as He has glorified Christ. In Christ, we have been given everything necessary to achieve our destiny in Him. His gifts and enabling are realized, however, as we walk in Christ, according to the model Jesus lived out here on earth. We reap the fruits of eternal life.

Jesus is the "pattern Son," demonstrated by His devotion as He dwelt in God's presence and walked in obedience to the Godhead. Jesus was given both the capacity to hear and was empowered by the Spirit to do His Father's will. This was the operative dynamic at work in Jesus as the Son of Man, who, "though He was a Son, yet He learned obedience by the things which He suffered" (Heb. 5:8). The encounter and engagement dynamic sets a framework for manifesting God's love in us, both willing and doing His good pleasure.

Since the beginning, this call has been indelibly written on the hearts of men, saved or unsaved. For "He has put eternity in their hearts" (Eccl. 3:11), i.e., He has placed a witness that calls us each to seek and be found of Him. It is the relentless pursuit of our heavenly Father, who often plays upon our heartstrings to woo us to Himself. The call is unique for each and deeply personal. My next chapter portrays this troubadour's song.

CHAPTER 3

ONCE UPON A DREAM

My beloved spoke, and said to me:
"Rise up, my love, my fair one, And come away."
—Song of Songs 2:10

Undoubtedly, the most poetic and romantic book of the Old Testament is an allegory set in a passionate scenario between a lover and his beloved. For a God who loved the world, He sent His only Son to redeem and form an everlasting union with His bride. As such, it is not difficult to understand that the bridegroom is willing to pursue His beloved even to the ends of the earth. As mentioned, God has set eternity in our hearts, an awareness born of the hope of fulfilling something beyond what this world offers. In turn, Paul on Mars Hill proclaims that God has set the times and dwelling places of humans so that they will seek the Lord in the hope of finding Him (Acts 17:26–27).

It is the Father's heart to capture the hearts of those He loves. He never ceases to pursue us and draw us to Himself. I can't help but compare this idea to a scene from the Song of Solomon—a love story where the hearts of distant lovers become desperate for their union. The story has all the romance of a passionate French novel, where the desire between a lover and his beloved tugs at the reader's heartstrings. The account is a metaphor for what the apostle John wrote: "What great love the Father has lavished on us, that we should be called children of God!" (1 John 3:1 NIV). Who is the lover and the beloved? The Bible tells us it's not that we first loved Him but that He first loved us (1 John 4:10). He longs to be joined with us and to dwell in us. What a sacrifice He was willing to endure that we would be made one in His love.

Although many have sensed the call, not all have responded. Why do so few receive His election after so many are called? What longings, desires, and waters must someone pass through until they are willing to let the One who has given His life as a ransom access their heart?

In John 17, we encounter Jesus praying in the garden. The scene follows the Last Supper and is the final moment of conciliation He experiences before His arrest, trial, and execution. How does Jesus spend His time? Does He not intercede on our behalf? Was this not someone immersed in and sold out to selfless love? Having fully realized what was required of Him, He despised the shame and willingly gave Himself as a ransom that we might be restored and reunited with the Father in heaven. Is this not the most significant act a lover can do for his beloved?

We can vividly see this heart-to-heart connection played out as Jesus weeps over Jerusalem. "O Jerusalem, Jerusalem, the one who kills the prophets and stones those who are sent to her! How often I wanted to gather your children together, as a hen gathers her chicks under her wings, but you were not willing!" (Matt. 23:37). Connection, by its very essence, is where we engage our true lover. The beauty, however, is made possible by the One who keeps us in fellowship with the Father Himself. For Christ Himself is the mediator between man and God, and, as we will see, between members of His body.

CHAPTER 4

THE ANCHOR OF OUR SOULS

Up to this point, we've examined the connection between encounter and engagement as call and response, defining it as a link between two parties. From here, we take a more personal evaluation as a partnership and union between the one who speaks and the one who listens and adheres.

Encounter in a spiritual sense always involves one who initiates and one who receives. God spoke to Moses on the mountain and spoke to His people through the prophets. Jesus came preaching the kingdom. "As many as received Him, to them He gave the right to become children of God" (John 1:12). When God speaks, whether through the Scriptures, a spoken word, or in the still small voice of the Lord, there is always a heavenly intention from above. God speaks to us; that's why He is called the Word. For God has designed in His sheep the capacity to hear His voice, so that through communication, He may have fellowship with us as He had with His Son.

Whether directly through the Word or through one another, the Spirit may impart words of affirmation, comfort, edification, or exhortation. As the Helper, the Spirit may also provide us with an immediate word of instruction or direction, alerting us to safety.

God speaks to us; that's why He is called the Word.

Jesus, as the Word, walked in the Word of His Father. He declares, "I have come down from heaven, not to do My own will, but the will of Him who sent Me" (John 6:38). Here, we see Jesus, by faith, doing the works He was instructed to do. As He walked in faith, He was compelled to action. So, as with the Son of Man, we are called to walk in like manner. For it is by faith that the power and glory of God are demonstrated and made known in a dark and fallen world.

Something happens when faith combines with action. What is sourced in heaven now manifests in the earthly realm. Heaven always tries to reach earth. Faith is the dynamic force that releases supernatural empowerment in our lives. As His Spirit resides within us by faith, so too does the Spirit come upon us to manifest His presence through us.

As fundamental as the above discourse seems, some hindrances and issues can impede or distract us from the simplicity of our walk with God. His sheep hear His voice; however, many other voices compete with the still, small voice of God's Spirit. This ubiquitous profusion of background noise is intended to bring us uncertainty. It stands to reason that the kingdom advancing on earth must endure the challenges and opposition that have long prevailed due to man's disobedience. We live in an age where not all encounters are God-ordained and can eventually lead us to despair and destruction.

Continuing along these lines, I coined a term that has been identified as "acquired dullness of hearing syndrome (ADHS)," which occurs when, after hearing, we either fail to follow the leading of the Spirit or outright ignore it. Due to his cultural prejudice, Jonah, unwilling to take up his role as an emissary to the Ninevites' debacle, seeks to run from the still, small voice of God's commissioning. Ultimately, it required the digestive juices of a large aquatic creature to bring Jonah again to the necessary receptivity and response. The lesson here is that the predisposition of our hearts directly affects our capacity to both hear God's voice and respond to His call and beckoning. It is our trust in both God's Word and His unlimited promises to us that secures us in the redemptive plans for our lives.

In Hebrews 6:17–18, we see that God, wanting to assure us that His promises to us are guaranteed, gave us His Word.

Since God cannot lie, the testimony of His Word, backed by His character, is solid and unchanging. If ever there was a day when we needed to have our sense of well-being anchored on a rock, it is today. Every social, political, and moral value has come under the critical scrutiny and influence of a worldly system steeped in self-righteousness and two-tier standards. I might add that social standards will continue to morph at every new whim of progressive ideology.

Again, it is faith that anchors us to hope, grounds us, and keeps us from drifting in times of trials and turbulence. "Without faith it is impossible to please Him" (Heb. 11:6). How does faith, a gift imparted by grace, please or not please God? May I suggest that, according to God's design, it is through obedience that we inherit His promises and walk in a manner pleasing to Him? Walking obedient to His commands is an ever-exciting opportunity to fulfill the exploits He has destined for us in Christ Jesus. If ever there was one concession to make, the encounter/engage dynamic is certainly not dull.

Walking in faith is one of the highest callings we all have. It is the essence of Christ's life poured out into our lives. Far be it from us to say that faith is only for our devotional lives, whereby we give thanks, praise, and worship Him. Faith in action allows us to bless and serve others. Once the cycle of faith and action commences, it recruits, trains, and gives us our marching orders. Faith in action puts us in the driver's seat to win the world for Christ and manifest His glory as we shine as lights in a world desperate to encounter a living, loving God.

As we examine the dynamics of encounters in connection with God's speaking and our response, I want to clarify again that a heavenly encounter is a supernatural phenomenon. It is a divine bridge to earth that opens our minds to God's thoughts. What follows may be simply awe, as Mary responds to the angel Gabriel, "How can this be, since I do not know a man?" (Luke 1:34). However, her response is of faith: "Let it be to me according to your word" (v. 38). Faith is a supernatural endowment that enables us to transition from natural reasoning to supernatural awareness, realization, and empowerment.

By design, it is through divine engagement that we are yoked as laborers and partners with God, doing His bidding. Our active engagement is necessary for fulfilling His intention for His kingdom to be realized on earth as it is in heaven. Illustrating these two essential components through call and response, we deem it vital that the bridge stretching from God makes us aware of the need for His prompting. To advance, however, now requires wisdom. God's wisdom unlocks grace and provides the "ways" and "means" factors.

> *Faith, as it were, is a supernatural endowment that allows us to step from natural reasoning to supernatural awareness, realization, and empowerment.*

We can readily observe the "What's happening and how do we proceed?" from a well-known scenario played out in Acts 2. The Holy Ghost had just fallen upon some 120 devoted followers who began speaking in other languages, as given by the Spirit. To the amazement and perplexity of the diverse foreign representatives present in Jerusalem, their initial response was amazement: "Whatever could this mean?" (Acts 2:12). Peter delivered his famous sermon. Quoting the prophet Joel, Peter connects the present events to those prophetically foretold from ages past. Those who heard and bore witness at Pentecost were cut to the heart and replied, "Men *and* brethren, what shall we do?" (v. 37).

Witnessing such a dynamic event, which some describe as the birth of the church, men's hearts were convicted by the encounter and raised the question of how to proceed. We could interpret their response to such an encounter as, "How must we engage?" Peter responded to what they saw and heard: "Repent, and … be baptized in the name of Jesus Christ" (Acts 2:38). Peter, demonstrating boldness, gives instructions and promises an outcome for their obedience. Upon repentance, remission of sins is followed by the gift of the Holy Spirit. With the conversion of souls, a redeemed interest in apostolic instruction, prayer, and fellowship was displayed by breaking bread, hearing, and proclaiming the word. Thankfully, this story has never ceased to be played out and will continue until the Day of Christ, when He returns to claim His inheritance.

CHAPTER 5

The Operative Law of Faith in Action

> Truly I tell you, if you have faith as small as a mustard seed, you can say to this mountain, 'Move from here to there,' and it will move.
>
> —Matthew 17:20 NIV

In the previous chapters, I described faith as a foundation, a ground zero upon which our Christian lives are built and lived out in accordance with our destinies. An essential aspect of the Christian walk is overcoming life's challenges, setbacks, and discouragements. We realized that encounters are meaningless without context. In His work to grow each of us into mature believers, the Lord uniquely designs and sets challenges that require faith in action. Without faith, we walk blindly, without hope and vision, and are vulnerable to the enemy's tactics that aim to draw us away from our partnership in His eternal plans.

Faith ends when we don't allow it to be put into action. As senior pastor Bill Johnson has said, "Conceptual faith is the enemy of faith in action."[1] It is essential, however, to understand that sometimes action begins with acquiescence, but as we mature, faith will, of necessity, require boldness and perseverance. Enter the idea of overcoming faith. As is often the case, faith puts us in the front seat with our foot to the pedal, awaiting action. I love the exhortation, "To him who overcomes I will grant to sit with

---

[1] Bill Johnson, "The Mind Trained by Faith," *Bethel Church* broadcast, May 2021.

Me on My throne" (Rev. 3:21). This kind of boldness prepares us to reign in life with Christ Jesus.

Faith requires our compliance and agreement at this point. Faith is present in encounters but is void without active engagement. Whether it be the quiet reconciliation that forgiveness brings or the moving of mountains, God's intention begins with the impartation of faith. Faith, however, does not leave us alone but brings us into agreement and partnership with Him.

The act of agreement with obedience defines belief and distinguishes it from faith. In believing, our faith first sets heaven's intention into motion, where the kingdom of God becomes manifest. "I believed and therefore I spoke" (2 Cor. 4:13), well-illustrates this dynamic in Rom. 10:8–9, where it says that with the heart one believes the truth, and with the mouth, confession is made, resulting in salvation. Something happens when faith combines with action. What is sourced in heaven is now manifest in the earthly realm.

As fundamental as overcoming faith is, some hindrances and issues can impede or distract us from the simplicity of our walk with God. All His sheep hear His voice; however, many compete with the still and not-so-still voice of God's Spirit, bringing us uncertainty. It stands to reason that as the kingdom of God advances here on earth, the gates of hell will make their stand and employ pushback.

Even where the ground is taken, the occupation itself will suffer resistance while enduring the subtle counter-efforts of the enemy. As humans, we quickly adhere to comfort, convenience, and expediency through the agency of an all-pervasive multimedia barrage of information to which we are exposed. Advertising consistently identifies needs and keeps the public informed about the latest trends.

I once visited a street ministry in New York City. They had secured permission to set up a van at a street corner, complete with a fold-out stage and public address (PA) system. Although surrounded by crack dealers on a corner in Lower East Manhattan, people hung out the windows, eagerly listening with enthusiasm as the team members gave their various testimonies. The regular daily Christian routine pales in comparison to the experience of praying with many desperate addicts. Upon returning to our outreach headquarters, we gave our reports to the other team members. I recall the venture coordinator telling us that the battle for souls was never over, for "the gates of hell down here in New York City are made of rubber."

Undoubtedly, some riptides and currents disturb the peaceful waters that calm our souls and give us blessed assurance. Unfortunately, we have an enemy who has taken advantage of a fallen world to make inroads into our minds through the sins of others and ourselves. The enemy, a liar from the beginning, has played upon our insecurities and our innate sense of inferiority to fashion vain imaginations concerning the integrity and character of God. In Daniel 7:25, we read that "the enemy will speak pompous words against the Most High and seek to persecute the saints, change times, and laws."

It's essential to note that persecution doesn't necessarily equate to being burned at the stake. The battleground of the enemy is most often fought within the believer's mind. Through intimidation, assumption, and conjecture, the enemy has dulled our capacity for clarity and truth, even our God-given cognitive ability to hear His voice, beginning in the garden of Eden, when mankind chose to live in the knowledge of good and evil.

"A good fight is a fight you win."

In his letter to Timothy, Paul admonishes his young disciple to "fight the good fight of the faith" (1 Tim. 6:12). What is a good fight? A good fight is a fight you win. Later, in 1 Timothy 6:20, Timothy was encouraged to guard what was committed to his trust. So, how do we maintain our guard while overcoming?

The verse that has always been an encouragement to me is, "Trust in the Lord with all your heart, And lean not on your own understanding; In all your ways acknowledge Him, And He shall direct your paths" (Prov. 3:5–6).

As it says in Hebrews 6:18–19, it is the assurance of God's word, backed by His character, that gives us a sure word that serves as an anchor for the soul.

Again, it is faith that anchors us to hope, grounds us, and keeps us from drifting in times of trials and turbulence. Without faith, there is no hope of victory. "This is the victory that has overcome the world—our faith" (1 John 5:4). Hebrews tells us that we cannot meet God's most fundamental requirements without faith in God. So, how does faith, a gift imparted by grace, please, or not please God? May I suggest that, according to God's design, it's through obedience that we inherit His promises and walk in a manner pleasing to Him? This may all seem regimented and sobering; however, part of walking in obedience to His commands is the ever-exciting opportunity to do the exploits He has destined for us in Christ Jesus.

Walking in faith is one of the highest callings we all have. It is the essence of Christ's life poured out into our lives. Far be it from us to say that faith is only for our devotional lives, whereby we give thanks, praise, and worship Him. Faith in action allows us to bless and serve others. Once the cycle of faith and action commences, they recruit, train, and give us our continued marching orders. All being said, faith has its rewards now and eternally. For in this temporal existence, faith in action puts us in the driver's seat to win the world for Christ and to manifest His glory, as we shine as lights in a world desperate for an encounter with a living, loving God.

CHAPTER 6

BEHOLD AND BECOME

We all, with unveiled face, beholding as in a mirror the glory of the Lord, are being transformed into the same image from glory to glory.

—2 Corinthians 3:18

The word *behold* means "to gaze upon." It may be only a glance or a captivating moment, like a deer caught in the headlights; we hesitate while assessing what's happening and what action is required. It might be a reflex or the convergence of accumulated wisdom called to mind instantly. Though most have not seen an angel, or at least were not aware of such an entity, we should have beheld His glory by now. Jesus, in His high priestly prayer, says, "I have given them the glory that *you gave me*" (John 17:22 NIV, emphasis added). God's glory is demonstrated in those who are alive in Christ, as we have witnessed in our fellowships. The transformed lives of those who have accepted Christ and walked with Him bear witness to His glory.

Some would say that an angelic encounter or being in the presence of the Lord changes them from the inside out. Such an encounter manifests God's power with transforming effects. Many have experienced an overwhelming sense of awe, while some have fallen into fear.

John fell as though dead at Jesus's feet on Patmos. For those witnessing angels—whether shepherds tending their flocks at the birth of Christ, Isaiah standing before the altar, or Moses encountering the burning bush—what follows these heavenly encounters is an initial response by each character in a drama of paramount historical significance. Within each supernatural encounter lies a choice and a gateway to experiencing the glory of God. Even so, beholding Him brings in return a wondrous yearning of promise. Greater intimacy with a loving God is available to us by beholding His continuous movement in our lives.

Transformation is the key element here. The issue of transformation into the likeness of Christ has been permanently settled in eternity. In the natural world, a bride always starts as a child. Although Adam and Eve were created fully grown, they were created innocent. Equipped for happiness, health, and prosperity, they were yet neophytes. They knew that God had made every provision for their growth and development. Both Adam and Eve were given the commission to tend the garden, to be fruitful, and multiply.

> *"Much of what we need has been given to us, but there yet remain higher realms and superior heavenly encounters for those who choose to live in devoted anticipation and pursuit of His ways." —Bill Johnson*

Multiplication in my life meant raising kids, a formidable chore indeed. I'm sure tending the garden included keeping the animals out of the vegetable patch and attending to it adequately. King David advanced through trials and conflicts during his youth. Jesus learned the ways of obedience through the things He endured. Knowing that we learn through the clinic of experience and guidance, it only seems right that God has ordained our learning curve to be an on-the-job, learn-as-we-go endeavor.

It stands to reason, then, as we advance from glory to glory, we also move from present truth to greater revelation and in the knowledge of the ascended One. The difference between simply witnessing the presence of God and walking in union with Him throughout one's life cannot be overstated. Israel knew the acts of God; however, Moses knew the ways of God (Ps. 103:7). Our acknowledgment of Christ was never meant to be an introduction, but an ever-unfolding encounter, both in this lifetime and in the next. Amen.

Bill Johnson, in several of his sermons, has said, "Much of what we need has been given to us, but there yet remain higher realms and superior heavenly encounters to those who choose to live in devoted anticipation and pursuit of His ways."[2] Many are called, but few are willing to move beyond the status quo to the mysteries that await us in the knowledge of God. I've heard it said that living in the status quo is another term for the rut you're in. One might ask what a rut is. Is it not but a grave with open ends? Ouch. However, we can rejoice. Even when in a rut, the only view is up. As the prodigal son assesses his deplorable state, he finally bears witness to his conscience and engages in a penitent act of confession and true repentance. So, how does this same dynamic of encounter/engage present itself today?

Who has not come to a place where a clear direction is needed, a fork in the road where perhaps we hesitate? Who has not faced the dilemma of which path to take when the way is uncertain, whether the most frequently traveled or the one often overlooked? A place where due diligence may be instantaneous, or discipline may require further evaluation and perseverance on our part. I've sometimes wondered how people interpret 2 Cor. 3:18, "As we behold in a mirror, we're changed." Is transformation instantaneous, or does it move us along a progression of further adventure on the stairway to heaven? I submit, therefore, that if God is a verb, does He not call us to boldly go where no one has gone before, to step out into the stream of healing waters? Can one not hear the bidding of the Spirit? Come on, the next journey awaits.

---

[2] Bill Johnson, commonly quoted, head pastor, Bethel Church, Redding, CA

As it is written:

> Eye has not seen, nor ear heard,
> Nor have entered into the heart of man
> The things which God has prepared for those who love Him.
>
> —1 Cor. 2:9

CHAPTER 7

Choice, the Unescapable Imperative

The Matrix is a 1999 science fiction action film written and directed by the Wachowskis.[3] The first movie in the *Matrix* series depicts a dystopian future in which humanity is unknowingly trapped within the Matrix, a simulated reality created by artificial intelligence machines. Believing computer hacker Neo to be "the One" prophesied to defeat them, Morpheus, the leader of an underground human resistance force, recruits Neo into a rebellion against an all-pervasive cyborg simulation.

In the movie, Morpheus presents Thomas Anderson, alias Neo, with a dire choice. Neo is offered a Blue Pill and a Red Pill. In this now well-noted scene, a choice with two outcomes, each tied to fateful destinies, is represented by two pills. The Red Pill represents an awakening, but one that could be unpredictable and painful. Neo's world will be altered in unrecognizable ways if he takes the Red Pill, but he'll be made aware of the truth of the world. The Blue Pill represents comfort and security. If he takes the Blue Pill, he'll continue to live content but ignorant of his enslavement. Neo, the unwitting protagonist, takes little time discerning the moment.

We are sometimes called to seize the moment at such critical junctures. Too often, we miss the opportunity of a lifetime, failing to recognize the lifetime of the opportunity. At some point, all of us will face situations where the bridge is out, when we're at our wits' end, or when we confront dire and consequential circumstances.

---

[3] [1] *The Matrix*, directed and written by Lana Wachowski and Lilly Wachowski (Burbank, CA: Warner Bros., 1999), motion picture.

Not all choices are threatening; however, our path will determine our future relationships, careers, and possessions.

It is evident, of course, that the "Blue Pill or the Red Pill" is being used metaphorically here. It may be a decision about which college we are to attend or the acceptance of a new job opportunity that's at stake. It may, however, be a dark hour of loss or conflict that would draw us into despair. Considering the life of Joseph, the choices he made after being sold into slavery set him on a course stranger than fiction, one you couldn't make up. In the end, all things led to a fateful encounter with Jacob's sons, where the outcome of his life choices led him to proclaim that that which was meant for evil God meant for good, to deliver and preserve His people. For indeed, it is written, "in all things God works for the good of those who love him, who have been called according to his purpose" (Rom. 8:28 NIV).

The life of an overcomer may be a hard pill to swallow, but the Lord shall grant the overcomers the ability to sit at His feet. Although our choices might have unforeseen outcomes, trust that God's plans are for good, not calamity. It's only after you've had ample experience and some degree of loss or disappointment that you will discover that the Red Pill is your best option. At the crux of difficult decisions, wisdom from above will rescue us from being trapped in predictability or being blocked and unable to progress toward our unique personal dreams.

Too often, we miss the opportunity of a lifetime, failing to recognize the lifetime of the opportunity.

Why the bunny trail concerning blue and red pills? As we return to biblical analogies, the question should not be what the Red Pill symbolizes, but *who* it represents. Red represents the shed blood of Christ. Through His shed blood, our transgressions have been removed, and we have been set free. For freedom's sake, you have been set free in Christ, not to be entangled with the ties that bind us. For those of little faith, the Blue Pill may well be illustrated by a life where the results of our plans and efforts run contrary to our best intentions and produce little fruit.

Throughout the Bible, however, many have been caught in the struggle of which pill they would choose. In Luke 18, Jesus tells the story of a wealthy young man's battle with self-sufficiency and personal pride. He describes the rich young ruler's dilemma between following Jesus and relying on himself. Jesus essentially offered him the Red Pill. Much to his chagrin, his worldly security, based on uncertain riches, left him distraught and sad. Although still rich, he is further dispossessed of redemptive blessing and heavenly security.

So, to what or to whom are we bound? You may say, "Yes, brother, but you don't know my circumstances." True, but I know God knows. I have it on good authority that He knows even more than you. Thanks be to God that He ever seeks and makes a way for those who would receive Him. Is He not a "waymaker" whose relentless compassion to seek and save the lost will pursue us by any means to be found in Him? As for the Red Pill, it can be said that it will find each of us at appointed times.

The apostle Paul notes a man sitting along the road at Lystra. This poor soul had been crippled from birth and had never walked. Listening to Paul preach had such an impact on him that it caught Paul's attention. "Paul, observing him intently and seeing that he had faith to be healed, said with a loud voice, 'Stand up straight on your feet!' And he leaped and walked" (Acts 14:9–10). Paul discerns a moment of divine opportunity, and, with a loud voice, commands the man to stand. The Red Pill of opportunity for healing has found the man; he engages in an encounter, jumps up to his feet, and skips down the road on his merry way. Be assured, dear reader, that none are immune to such consequential choices. None of us is safe from the Father's efforts to conform us to the image of His Son.

CHAPTER 8

CALL AND RESPONSE

Call to Me, and I will answer you, and show you great and mighty things, which you do not know.

—Jeremiah 33:3

I have distinguished between devotional encounters and when God addresses our understanding to provide us with guidance and direction through imparted wisdom and knowledge, or perhaps a tender affirmation of love. A great deal can be said for the refreshing that comes from soaking in His presence. Walking out a life holy and blameless before Him will require divine dialogue, prayer, searching the Scriptures, and trusting in His goodness. This chapter focuses on our pursuit of God as we seek His response to our call. We are instructed to "be anxious for nothing, but with prayer and supplication, with thanksgiving, to let our requests be known to God" (Phil. 4:6).

Much attention is given to our looking to God for His provision. There are times when situations require endurance, necessitating continued perseverance. These can be formidable situations, not for the faint of heart. At such junctures, we need to look to Jesus, who, for joy set before, endured the cross on our behalf. This admonition was penned with the intention that we take courage, not grow weary, and not give up. Although the trial of our faith may press us to the point of exhaustion, the result will typically be far more than anticipated. In Romans 5:3-4, Paul explains how tribulation produces perseverance, which in turn results in proven character and hope. Hope is something you can take to the bank.

I would like to share a brief personal testimony related to the verse above from Jeremiah 33:3. I was pursuing a second master's degree in educational administration at a local state college. I had enrolled in an elective course titled Special Education Law. The course, taught by an actual lawyer, was highly rigorous and challenging. As one may or may not know, unless they take a correspondence course, people usually select study partners or a small study group to survive and succeed in the inherent academic demands. I recall several phone calls to my partner regarding our last case assignment. The question was a run-on, one-page document written in third-year law school jargon, complete with terms like "party of the first" and "according to the second party," and loaded with symbols like §§§; you get the picture. My partner spent no less than eight hours trying to extract a meaningful question. I was very tired and out of ideas. I had no choice but to pray a desperate prayer: Lord, I need to complete this assignment, and I don't even know what it asks. Somewhere out of the third heaven came the answer. How about Jeremiah 33:3? Yes, Lord, but how does that verse apply to the question of law? An immediate and resounding answer abruptly formed: "What do I know about the law? I am the law and its fulfillment, ask away." A quick but earnest prayer was made. I took a deep breath and began to read the page before me. What I experienced was as if a highlighter were outlining the cryptic fragments of a question. I almost shouted, "There it is!" I called my partner, who instantly agreed with my analysis. Within an hour, I typed out the answer. I received an A for both the paper and the course. God is good.

Isaiah exhorts us to "seek the LORD while he may be found, call on him while he is near" (Isa. 55:6). Have you ever thought that God wasn't nearby? I'm sure there are times when you feel God's attention is directed at other things that deserve more consideration than your concerns. Contrast this thought with Paul's admonition to the Athenians on Mars Hill, when he declares that the Lord is not far from each of us. "For in Him we live and move and have our being" (Acts 17:28).

Could there ever be a purpose in God withdrawing from our awareness of His nearness? Year after year, Hannah wept daily in the temple because she was unable to conceive a child. "The Lord had closed her womb" (1 Sam. 1:5). Why would God take such an action? I've always believed that some things only occur through our earnest resolve and prolonged prayer to God. Sometimes, only the heart that has been prepared receives the greater blessings God has in store for us. "Therefore the Lord will wait, that He may be gracious to you; And therefore He will be exalted" (Isa. 30:18). As it were, Hannah did give birth to Samuel, the prophet who ushered in the most glorious period of Israel's history.

Again, we might ask why an omniscient God would require our suffering to accomplish his purposes on earth. Perhaps in the courts of heaven, justification would require God to become like us, i.e., to take on flesh and blood. Contextualization being the key, the Father sent His Son to dwell among us. We therefore read, "Since the children have flesh and blood, he too shared in their humanity so that by his death he might break the power of him who holds the power of death" (Heb. 2:14 NIV).

We can take comfort in the fact, that although it seems the heavens are as brass at times, our prayers are getting through. Remember that God is always near to us, even when we may feel He is distant. Let us not be deceived by Greek and Western thought that God is impersonal and removed from us. God desires for us to seek Him and draw ever closer to Him. He is not a distant or unattainable deity, but rather a loving and caring Father who longs for a relationship with His children.

On the one hand, we have the first great commandment: to love the Lord our God with all our heart, mind, and soul, and the second: to love others as we love ourselves. Connected to the second commandment is the Great Commission, also known as the call. The call, or commission, was never meant to be an option. Jesus said, "I will build my church" (Matt. 16:18). That starts with a revelation of who He is, the witness of His indwelling Holy

Spirit, and a command to go into the world to preach the good news, heal the sick, and make disciples.

Going into the world, however, assumes one is an ambassador of a living message that demonstrates both the knowledge of and power of God. If we are to be God's boots on the ground, should we not first be prepared and confident of who we are in Christ and who is in us? Where do we acquire the knowledge and skills necessary to carry out the call? From whom do the soldiers in God's army spring forth and do the exploits? May I suggest it's the spiritual midwives among us, those who are called to give birth, nurture, and raise an army of saints.

And so, the call begins as each one looks beyond how God can make life better to how God can make our lives more effective. Where are the midwives? Much more can be written on the equipping of the saints, but for now, we'll return to the call.

Contained within this excellent assignment are both generalization and specificity, i.e., as you proceed, speak the word, and follow the instructions as led. As a general principle, we are called to walk in the wisdom and knowledge of our Lord Jesus Christ, empowered by the Spirit, and motivated by His love. "Sanctify the Lord God in your hearts, and always be ready to give a defense to everyone who asks you a reason for the hope that is in you, with meekness and fear" (I Pet. 3:15).

Being in the Father's presence and walking in the heavenly mandate, Jesus learned obedience while continuing to grow in grace and knowledge. To develop into Christ as kings and priests, we must understand the operational dynamics of moving from encounter to engagement. The Father desires to give us the kingdom and partner with us in bringing heaven's ultimate goal to earth. Through Jesus's encounter and engagement with us, our destinies are sealed, paid for, and deployed.

CHAPTER 9

Mirror, Mirror on the Wall

From his classic poem, "The Man in the Mirror," Dale Wimbrow portrays a man gazing into a mirror, taking stock of himself through self-reflection.[4] His sense of self-worth appears to be tied to his degree of confidence. The last line gives a dire warning for dishonesty or dismissal of what is observed. "But your final reward will be heartache and tears if you've cheated the man in the glass."

There is a significant difference between a mere glance and fixing one's focused and undivided attention while looking in a mirror. Consider the man who, after a divine encounter, walks away. "For he observes himself, goes away, and immediately forgets what kind of man he was" (Jas. 1:24). My question is, does the man looking in a glass see the image God created in Him or a tainted rendering of his unredeemed self, painted on a fleshly canvas by the father of lies? Our self-perception can only be accurately understood in the light of who we are in Christ. The first consequence after Adam and Eve's disobedience was that their eyes were opened to a distorted perception of themselves, naked and ashamed.

The apostle James presents someone with little regard for truth, lacking the capacity and ability to distinguish between expediency and deception … sad. Apart from a genuine vision that regeneration affords us, we tend to dwell aimlessly. Having been born again, however, we have gained enlightened perception. For "if anyone is in Christ, he is a new creation; old things have passed away; behold, all things have become new" (2 Cor. 5:17).

---

[4] Dale Wimbrow, "The Man in the Mirror" (West Palm Beach, FL: The Cromwell Publishing Company, 1934).

Praise God that even when innocence was lost, He planned to restore broken relationships and bring sight to the blind.

Too often, we have become insensitive to being "created in the likeness of God." We marvel at the fact that God wanted to share His glory and create for Himself a family that would be ever joined with Him in eternity. Through generations of the offspring of Adam and Eve, He purposed to raise up a bride for His Son. We know all too well how the enemy played upon the innocence of each. Through disobedience, sin entered the world, bringing its consequences of separation and degradation. Paul speaks out of compassion to the Corinthian church, in which he has invested much time, correction, and patience. He writes, "But I fear, lest somehow, as the serpent deceived Eve by his craftiness, so your minds may be corrupted from the simplicity that is in Christ" (2 Cor. 11:3). Paul sees with a father's heart. This bride can be easily deceived while tolerating the foolishness of those preaching a false doctrine. He appeals to the believers in Galatia to turn away from those who preach a different gospel (Gal. 1:8).

As I have mentioned elsewhere, it is the ploy of the enemy to present lies concerning the Father's thoughts toward us, so that we become disenchanted and disassociated from a loving God. How often do we become preoccupied and forget the manner of love that has been bestowed upon us, which should call us into divine sonship?

God told Ezekiel to say what he saw in the vision of the valley of dry bones. The purpose of beholding the bones was to make a quick observation, process what he perceived, and engage in a prophetic act of proclamation. God required a prophet, representative of both heaven and earth, to release upon Israel His divine purpose. In this case, God limited His hand upon Israel through a partnership with Ezekiel. "The hand of the Lord came upon me and brought me out in the Spirit of the Lord, and set me down in the midst of the valley" (Ezek. 37:1). We will see later, when walking in the Spirit, that there are times of encounter when we may offer to God prayers of discerned needs for reconciliation, healing, provision, and blessing. We are instructed by Paul not to be overly burdened, but rather to bring our needs to the Father's attention through prayer and supplication. I would emphasize that effective prayer begins in the heart of God, expressly to instigate partnership and blessing on His part.

Consider the account in Acts 4 where this dynamic is in operation. The disciples had been beaten and released after publicly testifying to Christ. Counting it all joy to suffer for their Savior, they requested prayers upon deciding to return to the dangers of street ministry, their conviction being that God would hear their prayers, see their actions, and stretch forward His hand to confirm their actions with signs and wonders. In Acts 2:41, it says about three thousand souls were added to the church. From then on, beginning in Acts 6:7 and continuing in Acts 12:24, it is mentioned that the number of those believing the Word of God multiplied.

Here, we see a level of redemption that should give us a new incentive. As we grow and develop in hearing, beholding, and moving in the Spirit, greater exploits and extraordinary events will become the ordinary; to use an overstated cliché, it becomes the new normal.

CHAPTER 10

Hallways, Bridges, and Distant Doorways

I am the way and the truth and the life.

—John 14:6 NIV

By design, it is through repeated encounters and engagement that we participate together as co-laborers with Christ. Growing up into Christ, however, will necessitate perseverance and enduring faith. We can conclude that certain lifetime occupations may require years of time and investment. Regarding personal growth, desired outcomes are not instantaneous, especially regarding roles such as parenting or spiritual development for pastoral counseling. The encounter/engagement dynamic will require patience and trust throughout these long-term goals. James admonishes us, "Therefore be patient, brethren, until the coming of the Lord. See how the farmer waits for the precious fruit of the earth, waiting patiently for it until it receives the early and latter rain" (James 5:7). Let it be said that maturity does not come through the laying on of hands, but as fruit to be cultivated and grown.

The bridge to our destinies extends from where God breaks in on our lives. The path of our legacies may seem prolonged, fraught with setbacks, or simply confusing at times. The hopeful outcomes we seek may have even passed us by. It has been said that when God closes one door, He opens another. Little is said, however, concerning the hallway transition between where I am in life's journey and where I will one day finish. I recall a sermon by Jon Purkey, who delivered a message entitled "Hell in the

Hallway."⁵ He depicted the struggle often encountered along the dusty road as we embark on the journey from where we are in life to the aspirations we seek. He asserts that whenever we are called to a new season, God intentionally places obstacles and battles before us to win before we attain our ultimate victories. In a nutshell, pursuing dreams and destiny will require a fight. Why would the Almighty choose such tactics as disappointment and discouragement to impose themselves even on our best days? Recall Abraham, the father of our faith, who, against all hope, believed in hope (Rom. 4:18). It was an example of how Abraham, through holy tenacity, based on a divine promise, grew in confidence despite the impossibility of the situation. Consider that Jesus, while walking out the plan His Father had set before Him, had to endure much opposition in the days of His flesh.

Taking ground in the kingdom will always bring opposition. Sometimes, distractions come in the form of voices spoken along the way. We are reminded of past failures, real or imagined, that slow down or even halt our progress. The enemy is seldom concerned about where we are as long as we don't move into his territory. We can wear the enemy out and send him on his way by resisting the devil and remaining steadfast in our faith. We should, therefore, take solace in knowing that problems will have the power to bring promotion if we hold to His promises.

It is important to consider the question of why God uses opposition and the enemy's tactics to further His cause. Walking through the valley of doubtful disputations is where our resolve is tested and proven, while faith is perfected. It is the trying of our patience that produces faith (James 1:3). Consider Jesus, led by the Spirit, who entered the wilderness to be tempted and tried. Did He not encounter hell along the way? He may have begun His ordeal with potential, but ultimately, He emerged in power.

---

⁵ Jon Purkey, "Hell in the Hallway: Navigating Transitions with Encouragement and Faith" *YouTube video*, posted Aug 6, 2023, length 1:31:49, https://www.youtube.com/watch?v=s4V-9Bb13Hs.

It's essential to remember how in perseverance, one wins one's soul (Luke 21:19). The overcomer must remember that God intends to have mature saints who are thoroughly persuaded that He intends to carry out what He has promised. As Jesus walked along the way during His sojourn, we see where Jesus instructs His disciples that His church would be built upon Peter's confession of faith. The scene takes place at Caesarea Philippi, where a huge rock partially covered the entrance to what was believed to be the underworld, a gateway to where demons were thought to reside—in other words, the "gates of hell." In addition to Peter's revelation of Christ, keys would also be given. Such keys would be necessary to unpack kingdom dominance and thwart the advance of hell itself. The "master key," however, the indwelling Spirit, was later granted on the day of Pentecost—a gift unparalleled that would forever change history. Jesus spoke of the Holy Spirit in Jn.14:26 saying, "the Helper, the Holy Spirit, whom the Father will send in My name, He will teach you all things, and bring to your remembrance all things that I said to you." Although our journeys may vary, we will all be grateful upon arriving at our destinations, having acquired more than we bargained for "eye has not seen, nor ear heard, Nor have entered into the heart of man The things which God has prepared for those who love Him" (I Cor.2:9).

CHAPTER 11

As You Go

A long, dusty road denotes a journey fraught with inconvenience and discomfort. Although undertaken with hopes, the excursion may fail to resolve unfulfilled questions of purpose and meaning. I can't help but compare this theme to John Bunyan's classic novel *The Pilgrim's Progress*. The book is an epic, allegorical tale about an adventurous young man who embarks on a journey from a place of desperation to a heavenly abode. Along the way, the central figure encounters various spiritual trials and tribulations as he strives to remain steadfast in his beliefs. *Pilgrim's Progress* should be required reading for those desiring to advance in their quest for kingdom exploits.

In a letter to the Philippians, Paul recounts his worldly accomplishments and accolades to be garbage compared to knowing Christ (Phil. 3:8). As he had initially set out from Jerusalem to Samaria with permission to arrest believers, he was knocked to the ground, blinded, and was led by the hand to Damascus, where his sight was restored. Many feared Saul and sought to harm him. Even upon his escape, he was later stoned. He was rescued and fled, seeking asylum in Tarsus. Later, Paul recounts his many trials but never strays from the vision he was called to. He resolves to press on, that he may lay hold of that for which Christ Jesus had also laid hold of him (Phil. 3:12).

Each of us is called to a personal journey: He "has saved us and called *us* with a holy calling, not according to our works, but according to His own purpose and grace which was given to us in Christ Jesus before time began" (2 Tim. 1:9). So, we're all called to get on board, even if the destination may not be clear as we depart for our destinations. The Great Commission details the highest call appointed to Christ's bride, but does not specify where to end up in the journey. John records the words of Jesus: "I chose you and appointed you that you should go and bear fruit, and *that* your fruit should remain" (John 15:16). Implied in the mandate is that fruit is to bear fruit. Several times in Genesis 1, God proclaims that every living thing He creates should multiply after its kind, thus reproducing the nature and characteristics of the parent species. Using the Genesis account as an allegory, we see that Jesus builds upon the idea of replication as He labors among His disciples. From feeding the multitudes, spreading the word, and working miracles, He devotes almost every recorded moment to investing in a chosen people who are trained to launch a worldwide quest to preach the gospel to every creature, accompanied by signs and wonders.

Upon Jesus's ascension, He distributed gifts to equip the saints for ministry (Eph. 4:8). Each gift is identified by the working of each unique attribute, equally functioning in Jesus but distributed according to the grace operating through individuals. Each one, however, is called to present the message of salvation, welcome new converts, bless them, and raise disciples. We will be presented with divine encounters and share good news with others throughout our journeys. Paul explains how "you also have become dead to the law through the body of Christ, that you may be married to another—to Him who was raised from the dead, that we should bear fruit to God" (Rom. 7:4). May we all have fruitful journeys along the way. The invitation to journey with God should not merely be a mandate. The journey each of us is called to offers life's most significant fulfillment. It is time for excitement, mystery, and discovery. A time that God Himself looks forward to partnering with and walking out with us. I once had the author Graham Cooke autograph one of his books for me. He wrote inside the cover, "Enjoy the journey, as much as God enjoys the journey with you." Amen.

Whether commandments or commission, whatever things Jesus assigned us, He also makes us capable of completing the task, despite our weaknesses. We carry out His will according to the effectual working of His Spirit, which abides in us. I often recall the elder prophet who fathered me in the faith in my early years. He would frequently say that God's commands are God's enablements. In other words, the wonderful thing about God's commandments in the New Testament is that whatever He requires of us, He also makes us capable of accomplishing, despite our weaknesses.

It's a relatively simple process whereby, led by the Spirit, we are given direction and empowerment to accomplish heaven's requests. Our part is to believe, engage, and walk. When the disciples asked Jesus how they might do the works of God, Jesus responded, "The work of God is this: to believe in the one he has sent" (John 6:29).

Something comes alive when the word of faith is put into action, and we continue walking in what we've been called to do. Paul speaks to the church he planted in Philippi, saying, "The things which you learned and received and heard and saw in me, these do, and the God of peace will be with you" (Phil. 4:9). What a remedy for present anxiety. Besides the day's events intruding upon us, we continually face personal decisions requiring our attention. What an assurance that He never leaves us or forsakes His beloved, but watches over us constantly.

> Trust in and rely confidently on the Lord with all your heart
> And do not rely on your own insight or understanding.
> In all your ways know and acknowledge and recognize Him,
> And He will make your paths straight and smooth
> [removing obstacles that block your way].
> —Prov. 3:5–6 AMP

The wonderful thing about God's commandments in the New Testament is that whatever He requires of us, He also makes us capable of accomplishing despite our weaknesses.

The call to His church is both corporate and individual. "He chose us in Him before the foundation of the world, that we should be holy and without blame before Him in love, having predestined us to adoption as sons by Jesus Christ to Himself, according to the good pleasure of His will" (Eph. 1:4–5). This corporate call speaks to God's intention for all His children. It is God's eternal purpose for man. Still, as members of the body of Christ, we are "members individually" (1 Cor. 12:27). Jesus called each of His disciples by name, so He has called each of us individually. For each, He has set a time, place, and calling. To each of us, He has equipped us for the journey. Scripture clearly states the overarching vision for Christ's church. We each have a valued place in this master plan's economy. However, I submit that the journey's challenges for each will require our assessments, personal visions, and commitments. To press on to the high callings of God in Christ calls everyone, but we must engage and apprehend them for ourselves.

My early journey in Christ many years ago was undoubtedly life-changing. I reveled in the Word, joined in fellowship, and experienced great worship. I began to seek my participation in church and became aware that God had given me a specific calling and gifts. I found that my voice was designed to share what I was learning. My roommate at the time had been a brilliant student from Holy Cross University and later attended Columbia University in New York City. We would often dialogue into the late hours over the latest biblical insights and newest revelations. Yet, I still needed the Father of lights to break in occasionally with a personal word and direction for my life.

At that time, we received in-depth teachings on Ephesians 4, including the five-fold ministry and other spiritual gifts. At the conclusion, we had a presbytery of leaders who called out those they believed were marked with sure gifts. I was almost knocked out of my pew when the senior prophet called me up and proclaimed that God had called me to be a teacher. A few years later, at a distant prophetic conference, I was again called out to not only teach the Word but to minister the Word. Little did I know then, but what followed later was the release of prophetic gifting.

As the journey began, my first outings did not bode well. I was young, heady, wordy, and downright too conceptual, a trait I still need to work on, as the reader might have guessed. The gifts of God, however, are without repentance. What has begun in Christ, He has every intention of perfecting. As marriage, children, various occupations, and financial hardships followed, the Holy Spirit, through life's circumstances, guided me through several learning curves of His design. Eventually, I returned to college and graduate school, where I learned to organize, focus, and present my ideas effectively. In hindsight, the wisdom of the Spirit's itinerary has become clear for what it was: exactly what I needed. A gift may be imparted, but a ministry must be developed over time, through events, and by persevering through it all.

---

*What has begun in Christ,
He has every intention of perfecting.*

So, what do we do with encounters? We thank Him for His insight and promptness, and we pursue His wisdom, walking under His leadership. Sometimes the Lord seems near and easy to find (a good time to call upon Him); sometimes it takes prayer and perseverance, not to mention the counsel of those will support you, help bear your burden, and aid you in completing your assignment.

At this juncture in the journey, I've realized the Father's heart from different perspectives. Just as I've seen my sons grow and flourish, along with some timely counsel, I gained insight into how my Father has enjoyed the journey with me. I believe everyone, including myself, should nurture greater appreciation and learn to enjoy the journey as our heavenly Father does with us. Bon voyage.

CHAPTER 12

Cleanup Time

The fear of the Lord is clean, enduring forever.

—Psalm 19:9

Another operative factor within the encounter/engagement dynamic is wisdom. Wisdom puts context to our knowledge, guiding when and how to speak and act. Wisdom sets the boundaries of God's redemptive power and connects heaven to earth in the present moment. "But to those whom God has called, both Jews and Greeks, Christ the power of God and the wisdom of God" (1 Cor. 1:24 NIV). The abiding Spirit within us bears witness to God's love and leads us to paths of righteousness. The night before His crucifixion, Jesus prayed to the Father to send a helper, even the Spirit of truth (John 14:17). This would be the One who would both encounter, engage, and empower us to fulfill the purposes for which Jesus was sent. When we discuss the agency of the Holy Spirit, it is essential to understand that the Spirit resides within us for our comfort and guidance, and rests upon us for service and to bless others. The Spirit cleanses us from the consequences of unbelief and sinful behavior and leads us to walk in God's will. "And to her it was granted to be arrayed in fine linen, clean and bright, for the fine linen is the righteous acts of the saints" (Rev. 19:8).

We discussed fear as a destructive force that leads to separation and sin. However, godly fear can correct, direct, and protect us. Godly fear will always prevail over the devil and outwit him at his own game. Solomon tells us that godly fear is based on a promise written in Proverbs 9:10: "The fear of the Lord is the beginning of wisdom." Wisdom ranks highest when apprehending the mind of God. "But the wisdom that is from above is first pure, then peaceable, gentle, willing to yield, full of mercy and good fruits, without partiality and without hypocrisy" (James 3:17 NKJV). James recognizes that wisdom is essential for navigating difficult circumstances; it engages us in the revelation of God's purposes, which are necessary for spiritual maturity.

Speaking of spiritual maturity, I had a unique encounter regarding the power of the tongue early in my marriage. Do you recall where Jesus quotes Proverbs 25:21 concerning feeding your enemy? He says, "In so doing, you will heap coals of fire on his head" (Rom. 12:20). We've all heard God speaking in a still, small voice. There were times when it wasn't so quiet or still. After one verbal confrontation with my dear wife, I began to walk away when a distinct word from the Spirit confronted me: *The woman you are speaking harshly to is my daughter. Is this how you treat her?* Ouch! Speaking of encounters, what defense can stand against such an injunction? The Spirit had conspired against my flesh, undermining my unbecoming attitude. It's what I've often called a "blessed betrayal." This admonition only drives home that the kingdom of God is not just about being right, but also "of righteousness and peace and joy in the Holy Spirit" (Rom. 14:17). So, what will you do when your spirit aligns with God and says, "Go make it right, pal"? Can I say that knowing the right thing to do is moot if the right action does not follow it? A fear of the Lord prevailed and helped me clean up my mess. Oh, by the way, men, you're welcome for the advice.

CHAPTER 13

CAUGHT IN THE MIDDLE

The one who breaks open will come up before them;
They will break out,
Pass through the gate,
And go out by it.

—Micah 2:13

We sometimes find ourselves caught between encounter and engagement. In her book, *The Breaker Anointing*, Barbara Yoder describes a condition where many, for various reasons, become trapped in a place that renders them unable to progress in their faith and immobilizes them in fear.[6] In the previous chapter, I spoke of fear of the Lord and its godly benefits. The fear the enemy imposes on us stems from agreement with his lies, judgments, and accusations. Whether it is fear of failure, criticism, or just debilitating issues of the past, even the very elect will experience occasional lockdowns. Daniel 7:25, which I will elaborate on elsewhere, says the enemy's most concerted effort is his false account of the Most High, His character, and His eternal plans. In Hebrews 10:27, fear may be described as a "certain *terrifying expectation* of [divine] judgment" (AMP).

Fear was the first fruit of man's separation from a loving God. From that first moment, death reigned, and sin ruled. Adam and Eve's intimacy and union with their Creator were now severed; they were left as subjects under the authority of their adversary and forced to live in sweat and labor. It has occurred to me that the enemy has little concern for our demise; whatever cruelty he

---

[6] Barbara Yoder, *The Breaker Anointing* (Grand Rapids, MI: Baker Publishing Group, 2004), 46.

imposes on mankind is purely for spiteful revenge. Praise God that—through the agency of Christ's death and resurrection—grace broke the power of sin, death, and fear.

Micah 2:12–13, read from *The Message Bible,* accurately portrays the dynamic of encounter and engagement, highlighting the connection between them. "I'll get them together in one place—like sheep in a fold, like cattle in a corral—a milling throng of homebound people! Then I, God, will burst all confinements and lead them out into the open. They'll follow their King. I will be out in front leading them." Corrals are holding pens that generally house animals, such as sheep. Barbara Yoder describes the gate as a stronghold of restriction in this instance. It's a condition of demonic influence she attributes to a "python-like spirit."[7] She attributes the devil's power to immobilize us by deceiving us into believing in lies contrary to the truth that we are in Christ, the power of the blood of Christ is uncontestable, the work of the cross is finished, and the Father's love for us is never-ending. The demonic entity is well-named for its comparison to a serpent that constricts and squeezes the life out of its victim.

How often does it happen that when circumstances present a challenge, we don't stop to recognize the encounter at hand? Along with immediate awareness may come the normal intellectual response of panic. How often is it the tyranny of the urgent that knocks us off course? For the moment, at least, the problem appears more prominent than God.

Fear can be a cruel taskmaster, rendering its victim hopeless. Debilitating fear is the opposite of faith. It excludes the power of God's redemptive grace and denies His lordship. Fear only submits to itself and sets itself up as a god. Fear always requires obedience and sacrifice, yet ultimately, it leaves its subjects without hope or reconciliation. Fear, it is said, is religion gone bad, for it only adheres to a god who is deaf, impersonal, and powerless. The only

---

[7] Yoder, *The Breaker Anointing,* 46

trade-offs in worshiping such gods are self-deception, arrogance, and pride.

We are like sheep, living in the status quo; the instant an uncomfortable situation arises, we often rely on our normal, conditioned response in an attempt to bring us resolve for the moment. Sometimes, the rigors of choice can catch us off guard, causing us to daydream. We blink, yawn, and plod on. Too often, we get caught sitting on the fence in life, not realizing the fence belongs to the devil. We become the audience whose continuing passivity prevents any personal advancement.

When asked to assess Sunday's encounter, we will, without exception, say, "It was good." By Monday, however, whatever anointing we have encountered the day before has pretty much sifted down from our hearts and rolled out our feet. Too often, recollection of the sermon, or even a prophetic message and its impact, along with Elvis, has left the building.

Thanks be to God; this doesn't need to be our normal testimony. If "normal" means according to design, we ought to come honestly before Him for restoration, for He intends that we walk in liberty, in unfettered fellowship with our Creator. Let us not become dull when hearing the words that come to direct, correct, build us up, and lead us to victory.

CHAPTER 14

From Here to Eternity

From a spiritual perspective, many have embraced Jesus as their bridge over a precipice where they are only one step away from uncertainty and danger. Some may be afraid to step out, not realizing that He intends to carry them on His shoulders to the other side, for He is indeed a very present help in time of need. Jesus is the Good Shepherd who has promised that those who seek Him will find rest for their souls.

The classic song "Bridge Over Troubled Water" by Simon and Garfunkel has provided solace for many for years. For believers and unbelievers alike, there is much in common regarding human needs. We often find that even in secular writing, the love of God makes Himself known to those whose hearts are open to Him. You may want to read the following testimony with an open heart.

"Bridge Over Troubled Water"[8] is a poignant and timeless song that explores themes of friendship, support, and comfort in times of hardship. The lyrics convey a profound sense of empathy and unwavering commitment to being present for someone who is struggling emotionally or facing difficult circumstances. The recurring metaphor of a bridge over troubled water symbolizes the idea of providing comfort and assistance to a friend or loved one when they are in need. This unconditional support and empathy are the central emotional core of the song.

The phrase "I will lay me down" signifies the singer's willingness to be present as the person goes through challenges and pain, even if it means putting their own needs and desires aside. The final

---

[8] Paul Simon, "Bridge over Troubled Water," recorded by Simon & Garfunkel, on *Bridge over Troubled Water*, Columbia, 1970, vinyl.

verse offers hope in the form of where the writer can see their friend in the future—sailing forward and letting her dreams shine.

I find it difficult to dispel the humanity of Jesus evoked by the words of the writer of this commentary. The difference, of course, is the reassurance of eternal life. Such a realization alleviates much of the fear of death and makes heaven more appealing. "Precious in the sight of the Lord is the death of His saints" (Ps. 116:15). It is of the most significant concern to the Father when one of His children comes home. It is comforting to know that there are loving arms to welcome us into His presence at the hour of our departure from this world. It's nothing to rush, but it's reassuring.

Reflecting on our own bridge experiences, we should now find it within ourselves to bridge the gap of His care to those He has placed around us. In reaching out to others, we extend His hand and provide a loving encounter. It is the dwelling together in unity where God commands His blessing. Jesus says acting like a neighbor means behaving like the good Samaritan (Luke 10:36). Going and doing likewise could mean becoming bridgebuilders, whereby we extend the kingdom. Bearing one another's burdens fulfills the law of Christ, in so far as we are His ambassadors, called to be reconcilers and to demonstrate His loving kindness here and now.

As heaven intends to invade earth, God will require foot soldiers to lead the procession. As with the children of Israel, God had promised them an inheritance. Boots on the ground, however, were only the first significant hurdle. It's one thing for an army to take territory, but another to occupy and establish a colony, set up a government, plant the crops, reap the harvest, and defend the land. Once the swords are beaten into plowshares, a labor force is needed to gather the harvest and create marketing schemes for distribution. Building on this theory of economics and propriety, Jesus calls laborers into the field to collect the lost and those who build houses of refuge and celebration. There's plenty to do, and it's a call to action for those who hear the clarion call. Through our participation and partnership with the Holy Spirit, God has provided an unbounded capacity these days to advance not only the saints but also His kingdom here on earth.

PART TWO

BIBLICAL ACCOUNTS OF THE ENCOUNTER/ ENGAGEMENT DYNAMIC

CHAPTER 15

THE COURTS OF HEAVEN

> I sought for a man among them who would make a wall, and stand in the gap before Me on behalf of the land, that I should not destroy it; but I found no one.
>
> —Ezekiel 22:30

The chapter title "Courts of Heaven" may give some pause. Legal terms may be intimidating and complex, and best left to those with specialized expertise and professional degrees. In this chapter, we consider a different environment where the dynamic of encounter and engagement shifts into the arena of intercession, introducing our roles as tribunes in the courts of heaven. Although the term courts of heaven does not appear in the Bible, it is often associated with the idea of going before God's heavenly throne through prayer to seek justice or resolution in spiritual matters. Even the devil himself stood at the gates of heaven debating his case concerning the righteousness of Job.

The question we face today is whether the Father is yet looking for those who would stand in the gap for the kingdom to advance. Let's take a look at a legal proceeding occurring in Dan. 7:25, where the accuser has his day in court, persecuting the saints and speaking pompous lies against God.

> The court shall be seated,
> And they shall take away his dominion,
> To consume and destroy it forever.
> Then the kingdom and dominion,
> And the greatness of the kingdoms under the whole heaven,
> Shall be given to the people, the saints of the Most High
>
> —Dan. 7:26–27

Within our administrative role in the courts of heaven, we have been empowered with divine authority to legislate according to heaven's rulings. It is a continuing saga where the saints are called to a unique encounter where engaging wins the day and thwarts the enemy's schemes. Amen.

Consider the following excerpt by author Curt Landry:

> The Courts of Heaven is a real place where believers have access through prayer and petition, through intercession by the Holy Spirit, who intercedes for them. God governs His court system in Heaven as the sovereign Judge. He hears our circumstances and answers us according to His governmental system. Because there is a legal battle over the rights of this earth, there is an Accuser, and there is a Righteous Judge. The beauty is that we can come before the Judge, know His will, and petition in prayer. You don't need a law degree to understand the Scriptures; you need the Holy Spirit.
> —Curt Landry [9]

During the time of the prophet Ezekiel, the nation of Israel had fallen into apostasy and abomination through denial and despair. To prevent catastrophe and devastation, God sought an intercessor to stand before Him on behalf of the nation and avert its destruction. Moses interceded against the destruction of Sodom and Gomorrah, but to no avail. God sent the prophet Ezekiel to speak against their wickedness and turn them away from their rebellion, thereby preventing God's judgment. Have you ever wondered why He goes to such extremes to rescue His lost sheep? The simple answer is that even when God's people deny Him and pursue false gods, He never ceases loving humankind, for God is love and cannot deny Himself.

---

[9] Curt Landry Ministries, "What Exactly Is the Courts of Heaven All About?" *Curt Landry Ministries*, August 8, 2025, https://www.curtlandry.com/what-exactly-is-the-courts-of-heaven-all-about/.

God judges nations according to His standards of righteousness and His rules of engagement. The question that stands out here is why the momentum of God's hand rests upon the participation of human intercession for critical events in history: "Elijah was a human being, even as we are. He prayed earnestly that it would not rain, and it did not rain on the land for three and a half years. Again he prayed, and the heavens gave rain, and the earth produced its crops" (James 5:17–18 NIV). Whether it be Moses, Samson, or Elijah, God extends His authority to carry out His interventions through His prophets throughout human events. The highest of all interventions on our behalf was Jesus. "God so loved the world that He gave His only begotten Son, that whoever believes in Him should not perish but have everlasting life" (John 3:16). In a word, it is God's mercy, a mercy that triumphs over judgment (James 2:13).

Jesus states, "In the world you will have tribulation; but be of good cheer, I have overcome the world" (John 16:33). As we walk out our faith, conflict will occur. We, the saints, will be called to plead our case before heaven, releasing angels into the atmosphere to thwart the enemy's works and hasten the kingdom's advance to earth. Be assured that each will be subpoenaed for court appearances in due season. Praise God that we get to come boldly to pour out our requests before Him. Is it not through our priestly role, when subpoenaed by the Spirit, that we should intercede from the heavenly realm to earth? We should not take this call lightly, for "the effective, fervent prayer of a righteous man avails much" (James 5:16).

God first commanded Adam to subdue the earth, tend the garden, and name the animals. I am firm in the conviction that these responsibilities would have required Adam to seek wisdom and learn obedience as did Jesus Himself. The mandates were unfortunately put on hold when, through Adam's disobedience, the enemy gained authority on earth. Reinstated by the death and resurrection of Christ Jesus, the legal debt was satisfied and canceled, providing a means for creation to escape corruption through the coming of the saints. I love the verse that says, "The creation waits in eager expectation for the children of God to be revealed" (Rom. 8:19 NIV).

CHAPTER 16

Hammered, Heated, and Honed

> Many are the afflictions of the righteous, but the Lord delivers him out of them all.
>
> —Psalm 34:19

The promise of Psalm 34:19 is that God is faithful to sustain and deliver us from affliction. Affliction may come for various reasons. Sometimes it is we who have erred or gone astray, bringing consequences upon ourselves. We must return, repent, and confess our sins amid our troubles. Thankfully, God is faithful and forgives us. We'll refer to this as affliction by default. It is most vividly illustrated when Jonah, fleeing the presence of God, finds himself in the belly of a giant fish. Jonah realizes the cause of his calamity, repents, and is delivered. Jesus, on the other hand, is led out into the desert to be tested after being baptized. The affliction Jesus endured was a preparation for advancement. The encounters each experienced on their journeys allowed each to engage through obedience: for Jonah, a turning from rebellion, and Jesus, divine compliance. Each experienced the heat, was hammered and honed by their engagements, and prepared for their next venture.

For further insight into the concept of encounter and engagement by default, let us turn to Genesis 32:24–32. Here we see Jacob, a man somewhat entrapped by guilt and the misdeeds that followed him. Through the deceitfulness of his mother, Rebekah, an act of deception was used to violate Esau's cultural right of inheritance as the older brother of Jacob. Through this very act, a spirit of greed was released that would cause Jacob to work in craftiness and greatly hinder his ability to inherit what was rightfully his to possess. If you recall, the older was to serve the younger. Esau was enraged when learning the plot

Encounter God and Engage

that had previously robbed him of his birthright. Esau sought his brother's head and pursued him at great length to justify the crime. Fortunately, the story ends in reconciliation, but I would like to revisit an earlier event with Jacob to see how redemption sovereignly intervened in his life.

In his classic book *Daring to Draw Near*, John White dedicates a chapter to the story of Jacob's divine encounter called "A Crippling in the Chasm."[10] A night-long encounter took place in a ravine, the specific details of which are often misquoted but have strong relevance to the theme of this book. It's Jacob's story and about his encounter with the angel of the Lord. The story of Jacob in Genesis 32:22–32 is often misquoted and used as an example of earnest intercessory prayer. There are certainly times when breakthroughs may require persevering in prayer and fasting. We unwittingly misquote the verse, saying Jacob wrestled with God, as though Jacob initiated the struggle. It is yet another graphic illustration that a genuine encounter precedes engagement. However, looking closer at the text, it says, "a Man wrestled with him until the breaking of day." Please pay special attention to the word "breaking," as it is the quintessential event here.

The first question: Why wrestle? One is not bound to an opponent when boxing, as in a fistfight. With wrestling, however, one is physically engaged and may be unable to escape the struggle. The man is the Son of God, who, out of compassion, knows that unless Jacob is reduced to utter physical and mental exhaustion, he may still resist the intended blessings of God. Jacob's name means *usurper* or *one who illegally or forcibly seizes a position of power or importance*. God wanted to eliminate an enduring poverty mentality, keeping Jacob from the generational blessing, and elevate him to a relationship of trust.

Only in the desperation of a prolonged nocturnal struggle did Jacob finally have a breakthrough with himself. He finally

---

[10] John White, *Daring to Draw Near* (Downers Grove, IL: InterVarsity Press, 1977), 23.

surrendered to a fight of fright and became, at last, the aggressor. With daylight approaching and the purpose of the encounter fulfilled, a transformation away from Jacob's propensity to seize God's blessing had been broken. Jacob was now free to assert himself with a newfound conviction. "I will not let You go unless You bless me." What we see here was not just the release of another earthly blessing, but the process of adjustment that required transformation—a lesson to be learned.

The encounter, initiated by the Lord Himself, set the stage for Jacob's true destiny to emerge. In the exchange, Jacob underwent a metamorphosis that resulted in the acquisition of a new name, "Israel," and a repositioning of identity that aligned Jacob with God's purposes (v. 28). What did God gain? The advance of His chosen people for His inheritance—namely, the twelve tribes of Israel—to follow, and a significant advance in the lineage of Christ. Paul prayed that "the eyes of your understanding being enlightened; that you may know what is the hope of His calling, what are the riches of the glory of His inheritance in the saints" (Eph. 1:18). Ultimately, both encounters through engagement led to a win-win outcome for humanity and God.

Considering the spiritual process involved in maturity, there will be times of trials, temptations, and even tragedies that underscore our lives. For some who have suffered imprisonment, torture, and even martyrdom, we may conclude that Job had nothing on several persecuted saints throughout history. Jesus said, "In the world you will have tribulation; but be of good cheer, I have overcome the world" (John 16:33). It would be a safe assumption to say that the three Hebrew children emerging from the fiery furnace in Daniel 3 now possessed a more significant measure of proven character. Not to overspiritualize every tribulation, but weren't the Scriptures written for our encouragement, and that in times of being hammered, heated, and honed for the sake of Christ and the proving of our faith, they are more precious than gold?

CHAPTER 17

A Hospital of Hope or a Hospital of Despair

One of the most vivid accounts of someone stymied between encounter and engagement is illustrated in an account depicted in John 5:1–15. All too often, many get caught sitting on a fence between the two. Like a weed allowed to grow, hesitancy becomes deeply rooted and impervious to harsh conditions while competing with other beneficial plants. Using this analogy, the unredeemed thoughts, prejudices, and worldly presumptions we carry interfere with faith and our ability to overcome in times of doubt. As the psalmist says, let not presumptuous sin take dominion over me. The following is a detailed case study.

> Now there is in Jerusalem by the Sheep Gate a pool, which is called in Hebrew, Bethesda, having five porches. In these lay a great multitude of sick people, blind, lame, paralyzed, waiting for the moving of the water. For an angel went down at a certain time into the pool and stirred up the water; then whoever stepped in first, after the stirring of the water, was made well of whatever disease he had. Now a certain man was there who had an infirmity thirty-eight years. When Jesus saw him lying there, and knew that he already had been *in that condition* a long time, He said to him, "Do you want to be made well?"
>
> The sick man answered Him, "Sir, I have no man to put me into the pool when the water is stirred up; but while I am coming, another steps down before me."
>
> Jesus said to him, "Rise, take up your bed and walk."
>
> And immediately the man was made well, took up his bed, and walked.
>
> —John 5:2–8

Each one of the "multitude" present is described as impotent. The *Webster-Merriam Dictionary* defines *impotent* as lacking in power, strength, or vigor—being helpless.[11] Impotent, therefore, means unable to become or advance. In contrast, God has made provision through His Spirit, enabling us to grow in grace and knowledge. For "we are God's handiwork, created in Christ Jesus to do good works, which God prepared in advance for us to do" (Eph. 2:10). Frustration is often understood as a personal struggle dealing with an unresolved fulfillment. We only need to consider the frustration when wondering if our life's potential will ever be realized. I'm not just speaking of spiritual gifts, calling, or one's ministry, but the carnal mindsets that hinder the release of God's wellness or wholeness, whereby we are free to pursue His purposes for our lives.

Frustration, by its nature, is not inherently sinful or rebellious. Jesus was frustrated with Jerusalem for not recognizing who He was, the One sent by God to save and heal them. Out of frustration, Jesus turns over tables where various peddlers have physically blocked access to the temple, where the faithful have come to worship and offer their sacrifices before His Father. We need to recognize that frustration, when it turns to disappointment, may serve as a root of bitterness and eventually lead to unbelief.

I say this because it is essential to understand that unbelief is a spirit, and if left unaddressed, it will lead to spiritual blindness. Under the prolonged influence of unbelief, it will justify itself by blaming people and various external causes. If we are allowed to continue, even more serious consequences will render us dull and unresponsive to God's best. Sin is entirely conceived when, alas, we hold God Himself in contempt and accountable for evil intent and failure to condescend to a self-centered perspective and self-induced dilemmas. How subtle the enemy wearies the saints by misrepresenting who God is and His kind intentions.

---

[11] *Merriam-Webster.com Dictionary*, s.v. "impotent," accessed August 12, 2025, https://www.merriam-webster.com/dictionary/impotent.

Talk about fake news. This tendency is easy to recognize in the garden, when Adam blames God for assigning him the woman in the first place. Nothing brings someone closer to the road of perdition than believing the enemy's lies concerning the nature of God's intentions.

The rest of the chapter critically analyzes what transpired with the poor man in John 5:2–8. We observe three areas where impotence has taken its toll. After thirty-eight years, he was now blind, lame, withered, and in a paralyzed condition. As we read through these descriptions, we understand why Paul wrote in Romans 6:23 that "the wages of sin is death."

Blindness: "Even if our gospel is veiled, it is veiled to those who are perishing, whose minds the god of this age has blinded, who do not believe (2 Cor. 4:3–4). Paul prayed that the eyes of our understanding might be enlightened, so that we may know the hope of His calling (Eph. 1:18). Of course, blindness refers to those whose physical sight has been incapacitated, but also those hindered in discerning the moment or situation they are in. Those who have become dismissive of human conditions have been said to cast a blind eye to the factual situations at hand. Since all our senses are processed in our brains, the mind becomes hindered from facing life's issues. Sight, also called our spiritual perception, is correspondingly significant. Insight is a window into the soul; however, it is also subject to blindness, perhaps even more than natural blindness. The physical condition may be immediate, while the latter may be attributed to long-term neglect and misuse.

Lame: Here again, at the pool, those with legs existed, but they could not walk or progress. "As you therefore have received Christ Jesus the Lord, so walk in Him, rooted and built up in Him and established in the faith, as you have been taught, abounding in it with thanksgiving" (Col. 2:6–7). As we pause to consider the man Jesus is addressing, we see his condition has rendered him immobilized, unable to respond to wisdom, counsel, or instruction. Similarly, the necessary faculties that allow us to hear, respond, or advance might be absent. The idea extends beyond simply a lack of progress, recognizing that the opposite of liveliness is degradation and dysfunction.

Withered: Wholeness is the result of healthy connection and growth. When paralyzed or stunted by trauma, one is unable to make progress toward potential. Withering in Scripture most often means to dry up and fade away. For example, when grass is cut, there is no longer nourishment from the roots, and withering occurs during the day's heat.

The trauma mentioned above is not necessarily physically inflicted. Trauma may occur in any set of events where one is emotionally, psychologically, or spiritually overwhelmed due to threatening circumstances. The words of others may inflict trauma as an ungodly decree or curse. Trauma may again occur on different levels. It may be the result of an instantaneous injury or may result from long-term effects. Having grown up under an abusive parent may leave lifelong scars on the emotional well-being of a child. Many of the abuses we have suffered along the way have left inroads for the enemy of our souls to plant his lies. By whatever means, lies given or imposed have the power to deceive and disable.

To sum up the nature of lies, they are not always waged at directly demeaning the saint, but developing a false image of who God is, questioning His character, rulership, and word. Trauma usually works similarly to falsehood. Trauma is most damaging to the mind. The enemy seeks to rob, steal, and destroy. The effects of trauma do not go away. Peter was traumatized by his denial of Christ, but was able to repent and continue serving Christ. Judas, consumed with guilt, refused to resolve his betrayal of Jesus and ultimately reverted to the coward's way out and hung himself. Trauma, if not immediately rendered powerless with God's protection and sealed in prayer, will serve as an entry point for the enemy to establish strongholds that will adversely affect our capacity to believe in God and trust in His character. This limits our ability to reach maturity in certain areas of our lives. And so, it is now as it was in the garden. The devil plays on the insecurity and inferiority of the saints, creating anxiety while seeking to offer a solution that appears correct and profitable.

Back at the pool. The opportunity for wellness was not exclusive to one person at the pool. Verse 4 states that *whoever* stepped in first after the water was stirred was made well of *whatever* disease they had. There was only one catch: the first person to enter the water would be made well. So far, we have a snapshot of the overall situation occurring at the pool; however, we know that God calls each of His sheep by name (John 10:3). Although Jesus had compassion for the multitudes and wept over Jerusalem, He died for each one of us and desires to hold each of us close.

In John 5:6, Jesus begins to *personalize* the account by addressing a specific man who had been infirm for thirty-eight years. Notice that the following in verse 7 doesn't indicate what malady or sickness afflicted this man, nor does it specify how long he was impotent in his capacity to respond. It just says that Jesus saw him and knew that he had already been incapacitated for a long time.

If Jesus came and personally presented Himself to you, asking, "Do you *want* to be made well?" how would you respond? "Want" in Greek is *thelo*. The word combined with you is *theles* and has four levels of expressive desire.

1. Does one *wish*?
2. Does one *want*?
3. Is one *willing*?
4. Does one *will*?

To which of these does the man respond? It's important to note that the condition in verse 6 reveals a man who no longer has the will to choose. The devil had so eaten this guy's lunch that he had become unable to respond to the question, even though the Author of life stood before him. The delineations for the word "want" are of great importance when considering the level to which we are committed to engaging and standing in our resolve. I'm sure the disciples, on the night Jesus prayed in the garden, wished to stand with Him during His preparation for the events about to unfold. Could we assume that the disciples had imbibed too much wine at the Last Supper earlier, or perhaps they hadn't discerned what would befall their Master?

At least according to the Gethsemane account, there may have been a cap on the desire to watch and pray. After all, Jesus had the uncanny ability to walk through crowds unscathed. This may or may not beg the question, do we often lose our fervor or passion due to perhaps the cares of the world, or simply fatigue? To further develop this thought, Paul asks the Galatians: "Having begun in the Spirit, are you now being made perfect by the flesh?" (Gal. 3:3). Much of what constitutes a healthy attitude stems from a step-by-step, engaging walk that occurs as we partner with the Holy Spirit's guidance from day to day.

Unfortunately, the opposite is true. By design, life in the Spirit requires our will. We were intended to be sentient beings, fully aware of our capacity for choice. As we transition from childhood to adolescence and adulthood, we become increasingly aware that our choices bear consequences. Romans says, "the labor of the righteous *leads* to life, The wages of the wicked to sin" (Prov. 10:16). The ancient Greeks developed a logical system to interpret the natural world known as "cause and effect." We often observe this dynamic in both the spiritual realm and the natural order. How do we answer that if the wages of sin is death, how has the sentence been lifted? Fortunately, "[God] made Him who knew no sin to be sin for us, that we might become the righteousness of God in Him" (I Cor. 5:21).

Returning to our friend at the pool, he has been in this condition so long—through continued negative reinforcement—that he is now giving the Son of God his excuse: a well-rehearsed, totally justifiable account, based on his perceptions and self-deception. As demonstrated by his answer, the man has not only become blind, lame, and withered, but he has also become defunct of will. The man offers only excuses. It is what's called the "nobody/somebody" syndrome. I have *nobody* to help. In other words, the man waits for *somebody* else to be the key. Even when I intend to help myself, *somebody* else prevents me.

Does Jesus get involved with his excuse? Does he join our little pity parties? No, Jesus does not abide in my past or yours. He dwells by Spirit only in our present and future. From this perspective, His ultimate intention and your destiny, He prophetically calls you into the present and asks, "Do you want to be made whole?" I can't help but interject what I heard a preacher once say: Jesus wants you to know that He sees you in the future and says you look much better than you do today.

Going down for the count gives us a new perspective on the Bethesda event. It describes three instances of depression. Arriving at the scene, one needed to step *down* from the porches surrounding the pool. Many were lying *down* on the pavement, and all were waiting to be placed *down* into the waters at the appearance—or the encounter—of a heavenly host who would release them from their proverbial *down* condition.

What happens next has become a model for breaking destructive mindsets and unbinding the ties that have restricted and prevented saints from walking at liberty and entering the joy of the Lord. Some have called it speaking or operating in the opposite spirit. We have been instructed to pray for those who spitefully use us and even to love those who persecute us. In God's redemptive economy, He has called us to walk like Christ as we display His mercy and goodness in such a prayer. We can perhaps see now that Jesus operated in a dimension where light dispels the darkness, and His power is made perfect in weakness. We see this demonstrated by the physical, mental, and spiritual restoration of this man.

Wisdom and love of God are displayed as Jesus engages the man.

- Rise: Jesus looks at the man and says, "Rise." Jesus didn't only speak the word, but also empowered it. He was the *Word* and therefore put the *rise* into the man.
- Take up your bed: Jesus says it's time to carry what has carried you. He imparts the power to carry what He calls you to.

Taking His yoke upon us, He joyfully bears the weight for us so that we may, in turn, bear the weight for others.
- Walking requires putting your feet on the ground. Jesus was also giving him the will to do so. For it says in Philippians 2:13, "It is God who works in you both to will and to do for His good pleasure."

Looking back, we see that the defunct will need healing the most. As in the garden, the truth had been corrupted, and by his craftiness, the serpent had deceived both males and females. Deception is a spirit that will always target our minds and incapacitate our ability to believe in God. The net result of a defunct will is a passionless and impoverished condition, all too prevalent in churches today.

Summarizing: The deliverance demonstrated by Jesus brought three-dimensional changes.

1. To Rise Up: *A change in Direction.* All were lying down, and they sought to step down into the pool. Now He says, "Get up," This required a change of will, thinking, and directive.
2. To Take Up Your Bed: *A change in Dependency.* Jesus addresses the issue of dependency by instructing the man to pick up a bed—in this case, to carry what had carried him.
3. To Walk: *A change in Discipline.* Jesus knows that deliverance without discipline will not complete restoration. Restoration here means a change in lifestyle, a return to a regular pattern of responsible living.

Finally, back at the pool, the man does exactly as Jesus commanded. First, he was made well, then he took up his bed and walked. It was a decision of the will that put him into the recovery room, which was immediately followed by signs and wonders.

When the Jews asked who healed him, the man didn't know. However, his first response was to head to the temple to offer praise. Jesus then met him in the temple, confirmed his healing, and charged him to sin no more, lest a worse condition befall him. Here, we are given a clue that sin may have been the root of a thirty-eight-year gap in this man's life. To those who may adhere to biblical numerology, three is considered the number of God, and eight is associated with new beginnings. Through an encounter and engagement with God, the miraculous happens.

No specific sin is mentioned in this episode; however, the condition resulted from unbelief. Unbelief blocks the fulfillment of God's promises and His inheritance for us. The story concludes with the man transformed and hitting the streets to share a testimony of God's mercy and love.

CHAPTER 18

DAVID, THE FIRST ROCK STAR

The story in 1 Samuel 17 opens on the scene where the armies of Israel are gripped in fear and rendered ineffective by the threats of a formidable foe with a foul mouth. Why the armies of Israel condescended to a solution involving a one-to-one standoff never seemed to make sense; however, David showed up, assessed the situation, and called to account the inadmissible confrontation. He adamantly demanded to know why the uncircumcised Philistine was allowed to continue defying the army of the living God. David, having engaged in previous battles in the wild, had gained confidence that no fleshly obstacle or vile threat could thwart him. David shouted his intention to have Goliath's head that day. Looking down at David, armed with a leather cord and a small pouch of smooth rocks, can't you imagine the Philistine reciting the familiar children's chant, "Sticks and stones may break my bones, but words will never hurt me."

The entire story is a progressive account of encounters and engagement. In defiance, we see David walking onto the battlefield, experiencing a dynamic historical moment. It was a standoff between the armies of Israel and the Philistine champion, Goliath—the eldest of a vile and uncircumcised tribe of giants. Representing all that was worldly and vain, this grotesque creature had completely immobilized his opposition by intimidation and threats. David, a man after God's heart, found Goliath's defiance offensive and unacceptable.

We see in the book of Daniel the devices the enemy employs to wear down and intimidate the saints. "He (the enemy) shall speak pompous words against the Most High, Shall persecute the saints of the Most High, And shall intend to change times and law" (Daniel 7:25). The Bible says "we do not wrestle against flesh and blood, but against principalities, against powers, against the rulers of the darkness of this age, against spiritual *hosts* of wickedness in the heavenly *places*" (Eph. 6:12). A case can be made for the spirit operating in Goliath as he breathed out threats in an encounter with David. David, discerning the moment and filled with righteous indignation, seized the opportunity to engage Goliath and accept the challenge he offered. It was through the previous victories David faced that he gained the boldness and confidence to face and overcome such a challenge.

From whence did David acquire such an ironclad attitude and defiant response? Was it not acquired in the trenches of mundane and oftentimes demanding circumstances, challenges, and even threats previously faced? Fashioned in the furnace of affliction and threats, David successfully faced similar obstacles that test our resolve, sometimes to the limit. They were progressive and enduring challenges, each measuring his tenacity as he mastered previous lessons. The repetitive cycles of encounter and engagement that David had previously experienced had produced something in him that was forged in his soul, a proven character.

Paul related the high value of God's strength training in Romans 5 when he wrote, "We also glory in tribulations, knowing that tribulation produces perseverance; and perseverance, character; and character, hope" (vv. 3–4). It's a hope one can take to the bank, for it is well-established, certified, and backed by God's love. In understanding the regimen that God often subjects us to, we gain a profound appreciation for the knowledge that we are more than conquerors in Christ. David had no second thoughts, doubts, or double-mindedness, only a resolve that had been rehearsed and proven.

Some have said that David didn't know how many attempts it would take to subdue his adversary. I have always wondered why David chose rocks from a streambed for his battle. My conclusion, derived from my science background, is that the sharp edges of stones, subject to erosional forces in a streambed, become smooth and aerodynamically suitable projectiles. We're all familiar with skipping rocks over calm waters from the shore as children. Invariably, it was the smaller flat rocks that proved most successful.

Scholars tell us Goliath had four brothers, a tag team not to be dismissed. When David refused Saul's armor, having not tested it, he preferred smooth rocks that had been shaped over time. Rocks, paired with a sling, had proven helpful in matters of strategic defense. It may be interesting to note that God often employs such processes to shape those He calls to be soldiers in the faith. Paul admonished Timothy to "endure hardship as a good soldier of Jesus Christ. No one engaged in warfare entangles himself with the affairs of this life, that he may please him who enlisted him as a soldier" (2 Tim. 2:3–4). David's testimony becomes more relevant as our turbulent times require courage and vigilance.

PART THREE

ENCOUNTER/ENGAGE, PERSONAL ACCOUNTS

CHAPTER 19

THE MAN IN THE STREETS

> Pray for the peace and welfare of the city to which I send you, and you will know peace for yourselves.
>
> —Jeremiah 29:7 (paraphrased)

I have discussed how bridges of prayer, agreement, and pursuit of the Spirit's prompting bring us from encounters to outcomes ordained by God beforehand. Some years ago, shortly after my wife and I were married, we embarked on a venture across New York State with hopes of joining a new church plant. Having previously attended a church undergoing a problematic split, we were ready to pursue what we thought would be a new beginning with a church that opened its doors every weekend for evangelism. It all seemed promising until the visitors' attendance began to dwindle. At the same time, we found out we were expecting our first child. I needed to find a job and move out of the ministry house into our apartment.

Although I attended college for four years, I had switched majors three times and never completed a degree. I worked several jobs during the following years, including retail sales, hotel support staff, route sales for pet supplies, and as a representative for an insurance inspection company. I felt frustrated, not only because I had not achieved my professional goals, but also because I had a limited sense of God's direction for my life.

In retrospect, it wasn't for lack of aptitude or desire that I hadn't completed my education; I didn't have a tangible career pathway to pursue. This is often when men find themselves in crisis. I'm not talking about a midlife crisis, just not having much sense of purpose and lacking self-worth. Despite a loving wife who was willing to pray and offer encouragement, I came to believe there were times when only a father could impart what was perhaps missing. I longed for a mentor.

It so happened that the owner of the insurance inspection company I was working for was returning from field work and offered me a prime opportunity to work the territory where my wife and I had gone to college and were married. We knew several people who had joined a church plant in Western New York. Before we left, we attended one last service where hands were laid on us, accompanied by prayers and a prophetic word, "I'm sending you to the people in the streets." I wasn't sure what the implications were at the time. It was a word that would define my future calling and career, and launch my family, now of six children, in a whole new direction.

Moving to the inner city of Rochester, New York, had its challenges. Fortunately, children are early adapters of culture. They quickly made friends, played on city sports teams, and accelerated in their schoolwork. Several months after arriving, we had a guest presenter at a midweek church meeting representing InterVarsity International, which holds the Urbana Mission Conference every three years during the Christmas break at the University of Illinois. The focus was on reaching the unsaved, drawing no less than 17,000 collegiate students and various other groups with a heart for evangelism.

After watching a trailer about the upcoming conference's theme of urban vision and mission, I decided to attend, by hook or by crook. My pastor, a pro-mission enthusiast, and I, along with another couple, headed out on an eleven-hour trek across the mid-Atlantic states to Champaign, Illinois. As we embarked on this next phase of my destiny, I could only think of one word, often quoted by *Star Trek*'s Captain Picard after plotting his next course of action: "engage."

The theme that year was "Reaching Our Cities for God." The plenary speaker was Ajith Fernando, a Sri Lankan missiologist. He gave a fantastic four-day expository teaching from the book of Jonah. Jonah was the first evangelist in the Bible, who, fleeing the call of God, ended up swallowed by a prominent denizen of the deep. Jonah was a prophet called out of obscurity to preach salvation to a feared adversary of Israel—a nation about to be judged and destroyed. Due to ethical prejudice and hatred for the Ninevites, Jonah was not willing to cooperate with God's encounter or the role he was to play in God's sovereign plan for its inhabitants.

As we know, Jonah, whose skin was suffering from decomposition and who was trapped in a large marine creature, repented and, with great acquiescence, completed his assigned mission. When God saw what the inhabitants did and how they turned from their evil ways, He relented and did not bring on them the destruction He had threatened (Jonah 3:10). And so, Nineveh was saved along with its flocks. At the same time, the city prospered due to one man's obedience, even to the prophet's dismay.

One of the things I've experienced at a good conference is anticipating how my new vision will be pursued upon returning home. Upon returning, the couple who had joined our journey decided to invite neighbors over for campfires at their suburban home. I never learned how that worked out. As I pondered where to launch my mission, I somehow sensed that our neighborhood elementary school in the city held the key. I asked the vice principal if there were any opportunities to work with their Parent Teacher Association (PTA) or other parent committees.

Wow! Had God ever gone on ahead of me on this one. What had been slated for our city school district had been in a trial phase for various individual schools in the east. Known as "school-based initiatives," committees were selected and comprised of parents, teachers, and support staff. These committees were established to take ownership of decisions and special projects related to the needs of individuals with special requirements within our building. An election was held, and somehow, I was the concerned dad chosen to serve.

As corporate sponsorships provided financial and resource support, our school was selected to attend a week-long national training conference alongside others in our district. The week's highlight was designed to display what had been developed through the seminars and workshops of various speakers and presenters. Groups representing the administration, staff, and parent organizations developed specific talking points that helped create a framework for student achievement and strategies for school team success. Each team would then be subject to questions and answers from the other teams. State education officials, representatives from the National Council on Education and the Economy, contributors such as American Airlines, the Rockefeller Foundation, and several corporate representatives were present in the grand ballroom of a prominent local hotel where the conference was being held.

Due to my robust voice and readiness to speak, I was picked to help present on behalf of the parent team. We developed specific talking points, which, upon presentation, were subject to questions amidst the most enormous fishbowl of onlookers I'd ever seen. I had prayed earlier in the day for God to make me ready for such an encounter. Earlier, while walking down the hall, I overheard a question by one of the breakout session speakers. The question reminded me of a former boss's answer to a fellow employee who hadn't provided a customer with adequate information. The boss was quite emphatic when telling the employee, "If you're not sure what to tell a customer, you know me. Give me a call and together we'll get the answer you need."

One of our site-based team's roles was to assist in resolving parent and related school administrative issues. The last night of the conference culminated in a pivotal moment when an interviewing panel fired back a question: "Sounds like a formidable task. How do you provide practical advice for a concerned parent who needs reassurance and a solution?" God had indeed set me up with the same response the boss had given an employee years earlier. I marched over, grabbed the microphone, and let it rip. "I'll tell you what, if I don't know the answer to your question, I'll take you by the hand if I have to, we'll find the right people, and we won't stop until we have some answers." I don't know if it was the brevity, boldness, or conviction of my statement, but what happened next, I'll never forget. The audience jumped to their feet for a standing ovation that took my breath away.

With that, all seemed happy and relieved that the night had ended well. Many people came up and congratulated me. It was at that moment when I had flashbacks to the 1980 Winter Olympics in Lake Placid, New York, where a ragtag group of American hockey players had, against all odds, beaten the highly favored Soviet team and gone on to beat Finland for the gold medal. The arena was in pandemonium. I still vividly remember Jim Craig standing at center ice with the American flag draped around him, hoping to locate his father in the stands. Sportscaster Al Michaels, who had moments before shouted out, "Do you believe in miracles?" was now interpreting what Jim was silently saying. on the TV screen: "Where's my father?"

While people were still around me, offering their praise and handshakes, I glanced over to an empty side doorway of the ballroom. Although I couldn't see Him, I sensed that my heavenly Father was standing there, smiling with approval.

The word I referred to earlier was indeed a significant encounter. The engagement that followed had sent me to the streets, which could easily be symbolized as the City of Rochester, New York. I had interpreted the "people in the street" as the disenfranchised. As it turned out, the primary outcomes were about to take place.

Many cities have unfortunately become overpopulated with those disenfranchised and fatherless families. Here I was, having been moved from the suburbs across the state with my wife and several children, thrust into a city, and living in a rented house. A prophet once declared that I was called to be a teacher. Although I had some fruit ministering the Word, I never considered in my early Christian years that I would one day return to college, earn two master's degrees, and become a public high school and college science teacher.

The critical moment of the encounter came a year or so later, when a dear friend, now gone to be with his Maker, spoke to me at a playground where we had taken our kids after dinner. Twice earlier in the summer, on two different occasions, the parents I had served with on school committees had suggested that completing my education and entering the teaching field was not beyond a thirty-eight-year-old man's reach. Desire was present; however, the ways and means of such an endeavor remained a dilemma. How was I to approach, finance, or complete such a mission?

As my friend and I stood watching the kids play, he looked at me seriously and said, "Have you recently considered returning to college to become a teacher?" My mouth dropped open as he told me that he had been impressed by the Spirit during dinner, but with too much going on, decided to wait till later. He was impressed that God would open the doors and provide the necessary financing. It was now time to engage and pursue my life's calling.

I had heard of a state college specializing in correspondence that had an active chapter in my city. The next day, my wife called the college and signed me up for an orientation meeting scheduled for the following night. I have never been more impacted by the Spirit speaking through a secular voice than that night. So, off to school I went. Thanks to federal grants and numerous hours of study and writing, I completed the degree program in three years.

The Spirit had taken me on an extraordinary journey through numerous encounters and engagements to fulfill a significant life calling. The calling had not only set me on a course befitting of God-given design but also to bring my worldview to generations of young people. To my children and others looking ahead, my testimony has become an incentive and encouragement for their life pursuits, demonstrating the manifest goodness of God through an encounter and engagement relationship with the Spirit of God.

CHAPTER 20

ENCOUNTER GONE BAD

> I am jealous for you with a godly jealousy. I promised you to one husband, to Christ, so that I might present you as a pure virgin to him. But I am afraid that just as Eve was deceived by the serpent's cunning, your minds may somehow be led astray from your sincere and pure devotion to Christ.
>
> —2 Corinthians 11:2–3 NIV

Up to this point, we have discussed the encounter as a heavenly intervention or visitation, followed by a response and active engagement. As we well know, however, not all spiritual encounters are heaven-sourced. Peter, soon after being blessed by Jesus for having proclaimed by revelation who Jesus was, denies the necessity of Jesus's passion and crucifixion. As we see in Matthew 16:23, Jesus, discerning the source of a demonic encounter, turns and says to Peter, "Get behind Me, Satan! You are an offense to Me, for you are not mindful of the things of God, but the things of men."

Here, we see two sources of encounter: demonic and human. From the beginning, the enemy has been a liar, an embodiment of evil. Having been forewarned of choices and consequences, a demonic encounter in the garden of Eden led to a response. Convinced that the choice the serpent was offering her was a way out of the anxiety of the moment, Eve engaged in an act of disobedience that ultimately brought estrangement and shame. The enemy's craftiness had instilled in Eve a sense of insecurity and inferiority. Steve Foss refers to these two vulnerabilities in his book, *Satan's Dirty Little Secret*.[12] He maintains that all other sins are derived from these two fundamental human frailties through which the enemy has sought to bind, oppress, confound, and deceive mankind throughout the ages.

The deception and seduction were based on retribution through manipulation and control. In short, witchcraft is the agreement between the demonic and human spirits. Not to digress, but it is an all-too-common dynamic in our materialistic culture. Advertising has become an art that has mastered creating a sense of deficit, targeted at compulsivity to relieve a perceived need. This is easily demonstrated, especially when portraying a deficiency such as not having the latest technology, a bigger TV screen, or the latest designer apparel. Eve saw that the apple appeared to be good. She encountered and engaged, and the rest is history.

It is worth noting that God placed two trees in the garden of Eden. Although the two trees offered a stark contrast in outcomes, the choice served as a significant and defining opportunity in bringing Adam and Eve to a higher level of growth and discernment. They were innocent, but not yet developed in their faith. The Tree of Life offered them unbroken fellowship with God and provision for their quest to fulfill their commission. The other tree only honored man's moral capacity for choice and self-edification.

It was ordained from the beginning that man should live by every word that proceeded from a loving God. The living Word spoke to Adam in the cool of the evening. The evening is a time when the day's work is done, a time for satisfaction, assessment, and refreshing. Linkage had now been severed. Man's actions were no longer aligned and empowered by heavenly guidance. Unfortunately, humankind was sentenced to a life of blood, sweat, and tears.

If it weren't for the appointment of a Sabbath day of rest, mankind might have been consumed in his labor and toil. Alas,

---

[12] Stephen Foss, *Satan's Dirty Little Secret* (Lake Mary, FL: Creation House, 2007), 46.

Eve could only bear children through much pain; however, God granted her to be spared in childbirth lest her children not survive to populate the earth. That was crucial, for it was through the seed of Adam that God would send a Redeemer, the second Adam from above.

I used the previous scenario to show how and where our political institutions entered the world through one man's disobedience. Adam abdicated and exchanged a heavenly kingdom on earth for a fleshly and corruptible regime on earth—through the enemy's craft, a bait-and-switch had set consequences that would tragically play out throughout history. Adam ate the apple, but the devil ate their lunch.

As Solomon so eloquently wrote: "What has been will be again, what has been done will be done again; there is nothing new under the sun" (Eccl. 1:9 NIV). As we are painfully aware, the fallen nature of man has led to wars and rumors of wars, to conquering empires and despots that have robbed, stolen, and destroyed. In this generation, we have witnessed the dragon again raising its ugly head in our own "land of the free and home of the brave." And from his evil heart, Satan has subtly tightened his influence over the institutions and various major cultural venues of what Lance Wallnau and others have commonly termed "the Seven Mountains of Influence." [13]

Never has such political upheaval and polarization, fueled by media bias, corporate interests, and our new "woke" paradigms, made such a concerted effort to undermine the core values on which this country has stood and been committed to since its inception. Even within our churches, there appears to be a tolerance for what has been pounding on our doors. Not by necessarily condoning acts of violence, illegal entrance at our borders, and media censorship, but by maintaining the status quo of the church as

---

[13] Lance Wallnau, "Lance Wallnau Explains the Seven Mountains Mandate," YouTube video, 6:28, posted by "Bruce Wilson," July 16, 2009, https://www.youtube.com/watch?v=qQbGnJd9poc.

usual. Can someone define normalcy, please? Does "normal" mean something operating according to specification, or is it merely by popular consensus? God help us not to accept the latter. Were we not transformed to transform our world?

For too long, Christianity has been defined by a false concept of doing church according to prescribed norms. Leaders have largely relegated their efforts to preaching to maintain behavioral norms. Somewhere, we reversed the church's role from being the force to being the field. As a result, believers have built walls around their lives, keeping outside culture at a distance. Except for some modern versions of contemporary worship, wearing casual apparel, and a café dispensing lattes, much of our fellowship has little impact outside our four walls. Despite millions of God-fearing church members, contributors, and good citizens, how many saints go to bed at night with no blood on their swords?

All too often, we as present-day Christians have focused on keeping culture out of the church. Granted, our contemporary culture is rooted in Hellenistic and Western mindsets. We tend to worship youth and beauty, and our American culture celebrates perpetual adolescence. Unfortunately, the church has kept itself cloistered within its concerns. This was never Jesus's design for your life! Before the church was established as a place where people came to worship, Jesus instituted it as an outreach army, intending to bring about reform in society and to bring the kingdom to earth.

I wonder if the churches that have often instituted foundational series and discipleship programs for their constituents understand that discipleship, beginning at home, must ultimately spread outward, as it did in the early church. Jesus did not tell us to gather disciples, but rather to go and make disciples. I pray that God will raise up those who will fulfill our second commandment mandate. As in Acts 4, we should seek God for boldness and a voice that brings encounters to a desperate world on the verge of moral collapse. The church was never meant to be a field, but a force. No one should be safe from an encounter with the living God.

At the very least, we should realize that, as His ambassadors, we owe the world an encounter as the opportunity presents itself. However, as ambassadors, we walk in the power and demonstration of the Spirit. Therefore, it must be understood that we do not mishandle the Word, but rather, with divine guidance and seasoned with grace and mercy, we proclaim Christ.

CHAPTER 21

INNOCENT AS DOVES BUT WISE AS SERPENTS

Fools rush in where angels fear to tread.

—Alexander Pope

We must be willing to rise above, asking God to better our lives, but how can He make our lives more effective?

I have heard it said that, for the most part, we as the church have often excelled at the first part of our Lord's mandate concerning demonstrating the gospel. As citizens, we should contribute to community needs through volunteerism, relief to the disenfranchised, and maintaining open doors to our Sunday worship services and church picnics. We have been encouraged to be good Samaritans, visit the sick, encourage the brokenhearted, and feed the hungry—all good things.

Where many have not readily tread is where darkness has taken hold in our society, as earlier illustrated by Lance Wallnau's popular treatise on the Seven Mountains of Influence. There is much to consider in a role where we are still pioneers. Many do expect that the church will, by necessity, be called to confront the gates of hell and its minions that would seek to prevail against us. Such a mandate would require the emergence and alignment of prophetic warriors and intercessors to join forces as the heavenly kingdom presses down to invade the earth.

When I was a parent representative, I recall a time when the elementary school my children were attending had been approached by a group advocating Planned Parenthood's sex curriculum for students ranging from kindergarten to sixth grade.

One of their other agendas was to advance and validate different gender lifestyles as a matter of choice.

Since my children were attending the school and I was a recognized committee member, I realized I had the authority to pray, rally parents, and address this issue. Just a heads up: when standing in the gap for an entity in error, it is best to first repent for the benefit of unrighteousness within one's professional affiliation. Recall how God was willing to spare Sodom for the sake of a few intercessors.

To this day, I still must remind myself why God set me in as a public school teacher amidst union corruption and "woke" values. As I pointed out, we see—through propaganda, subtle political manipulation, control, and deception—the advancement of a trend alive and well on planet earth today. It only makes sense to realize that through God's call and response, we are made to be overcomers. There is no safer place to be than in the center of God's will. If we walk in the light, as He is in the light, we need not fear the darkness, but rather live assured that we will shine and advance His kingdom.

PART FOUR

WHERE IN THE WORLD ARE WE? CURRENT STATUS

CHAPTER 22

AGENTS OF DYNAMIC CHANGE

During the second half of the 20th century in America, an evangelistic movement was characterized by tent meetings and bold sermons delivered by fiery men who conveyed powerful messages reminiscent of John the Baptist's call to repentance. Conviction and a sense of God's disapproval drove many to the altar. The population had emerged from a worldwide depression. Churches had been a source of refuge and weekly inspiration in a society that generally embodied a Judeo-Christian moral consensus.

What had been implanted in the souls of a vast percentage of Western churchgoers, students, and even radio listeners was imprinted on the conscience of our culture. Even public schools of the day, acting *in loco parentis*, emulated a value base that encouraged honesty, morality, and a sense of national pride. For illustration, I would like to include a prevailing general agreement among our 20th-century baby boomers. It is known as the Scout Oath and the Scout Law, also referred to as the Core Values.

Boy Scout Oath:

On my honor, I will do my best to do my duty to God and my country and to obey the Scout Law; to help other people at all times; to keep myself physically strong, mentally awake, and morally straight.

Scout Motto: Be prepared

Scout Law and Description: A Scout is:

TRUSTWORTHY: A Scout tells the truth. He keeps his promises. Honesty is part of his code of conduct. People can depend on him.

LOYAL: A Scout is faithful to his family, Scout leaders, friends, school, and nation.

HELPFUL: A Scout is considerate of others. He does things willingly for others without pay or reward.

FRIENDLY: A Scout is a friend to all. He is a brother to other Scouts. He seeks to understand others. He respects those with ideas and customs that differ from his own.

COURTEOUS: A Scout is polite to everyone regardless of age or position. He knows that good manners make it easier for people to get along.

KIND: A Scout understands that there is strength in being gentle. He treats others as he wants to be treated. He does not hurt or kill harmless things without reason.

OBEDIENT: A Scout follows the rules of his family, school, and troop. He obeys the laws of his community and country. If he believes these rules and regulations are unfair, he attempts to have them changed in an orderly manner rather than disobeying them.

CHEERFUL: A Scout looks for the bright side of things. He cheerfully does tasks that come his way. He tries to make others happy.

THRIFTY: A Scout works to pay his way and to help others. He saves for unforeseen needs. He protects and conserves natural resources. He carefully uses time and property.

BRAVE: A Scout can face danger even when he is afraid. He dares to stand for what he thinks is right, even if others laugh at him or threaten him.

CLEAN: A Scout keeps his body and mind fit and clean. He goes around with those who believe in living by these same ideals. He helps keep his home and community clean.

REVERENT: A Scout is reverent toward God. He is faithful in his religious duties. He respects the beliefs of others.

Considering that these tenets were drafted in 1910 and endorsed by Presidents William Taft and Teddy Roosevelt, one gets a sense that the gospel profoundly influenced America in years past. The Boy Scout Oath was established as a rule of engagement that concluded with a mention of reverence. (It may be noted that both the Girl Scouts and Boy Scouts presented religious medals to those who qualified for notable achievement in church service.)

In Galatians 5:22–23 we have a list known as the fruit of the Spirit. It is what Paul used to differentiate between works of the flesh and Christly attributes that characterized moral standards available to us through God's grace and our engagement through faith as we walk in the Spirit.

> *"The fruit of the Spirit is love, joy, peace, longsuffering, kindness, goodness, faithfulness, ^{23 [a]}gentleness, self-control. Against such there is no law."*
> (Galatians 5:22–23)

As I look back. I realize what admirable ideals scouting upheld. One is authored under inspiration, and the other, through a Christian consensus. We can summarize both under an even higher commandment of love. "Love one another as I have loved you" (John 15:12) and "Love your neighbor as yourself" (Mark 12:31).

As you can see, the Boy Scouts had community support for spiritual values, although not necessarily a promotion of faith itself. Interestingly, I can still quote, after many decades, the twelve laws. We all believed in and attempted to uphold some system of moral values within our society, or at least had some indoctrination in them. Many had once heard the sermons or attended Sunday services in our youth. God's Word, never returning void, somehow lodged itself in our gray matter, perhaps waiting for a spark to ignite our future faith. Thus, when prodigals had come to the end of their ways, the spoken word could ignite a holy conviction, leading to recommitment and rededication to an earlier faith.

During the revivals of the 1950s, evangelists such as Billy Graham witnessed multitudes of conversions through the newly emerging medium of television. During the later decades of the 20th century, especially in the United States, a new trend began to displace the celebrated televangelists' style. A new generation of street evangelism emerged. Equipped with supernatural gifts such as the word of knowledge and prophetic insight, regular church members began to hit the streets. Since the kingdom comes not only in word but also in power, many took up the mandate that Jesus left us with, preaching and accompanying it with signs and wonders. With a far more personalized approach, as was the style demonstrated by Jesus, people began to perceive a God who knew them, one willing to show His love for them and demonstrate His power in their lives.

As previously detailed, an encounter is initiated by God. When responding to His command to go and preach the gospel, we aim to present the good news in our discourse, accompanied by signs and wonders. Our willingness and obedience, derived from the love of God and the Spirit, enable us to speak as ambassadors and empower us to lay hands on the sick, mend the brokenhearted, and perform miracles. Why do we readily call on God to perform when He has already done His part? Do we understand and believe He waits on high to act on our proclamations, declarations, and Spirit-led actions? Salvation, healing, and wholeness have already been accomplished through Christ's death and resurrection. Why do we continue to travail when faced with the perceived rigors of the harvest mandate?

These questions, though, are shouted from the rooftops to an audience that has become dull of hearing. What causes this deafness? Part of the answer is found in Hebrews 3, where the children of Israel, in rebellion (v. 8), fell into unbelief and lost sight of God's promise to deliver them and lead them to prosperity and multiplication. The writer of Hebrews then quotes Psalm 95: "Beware, brethren, lest there be in any of you an evil heart of unbelief in departing from the living God; but exhort one another daily, while it is called "Today," lest any of you be hardened through the deceitfulness of sin" (Heb. 3:12–13). It's a harsh word to swallow when attributing our dullness and lack of confidence in presenting the gospel message as we go, especially when we examine the causes of our deficit of unbelief. It seems that the devil has revived his emissaries in these days to distract and preoccupy us with other priorities.

CHAPTER 23

CALLED TO BRING ENCOUNTER

> Brethren, if a man is overtaken in any trespass, you who are spiritual restore such a one in a spirit of gentleness.
>
> —Galatians 6:1

Here again, the admonition given by Paul is an active word, providing us with guidelines for engaging others in correction, counsel, or advisement. We encounter the inspired word of instruction; when the opportunity arises, we humbly proceed accordingly. Our action initiates a divine encounter that offers reconciliation, restoration, and empowerment. When some translations use the phrase *a spirit of gentleness*, what comes through is the idea of preferring one another in love. I must point out, however, that this level of deferring involves two critical elements: our willingness and the Holy Spirit's enabling. Since divisions and offenses will arise, there is, of necessity, pressure and conflict in apprehending the kingdom and walking in the Spirit.

Author and speaker Danny Silk, in his book *Culture of Honor: Sustaining a Supernatural Environment*, highlights the significance of honoring one another in creating a culture and environment where a community of people learns to discern and receive each other in their God-given identities. When heaven is the model for Christian culture, the primary results are empowerment and peace.[14]

This cycle serves as a model of the connection between encounter and engagement, providing a pathway to growth in

---

[14] Danny Silk, *Culture of Honor: Sustaining a Supernatural Environment* (Shippensburg, PA: Destiny Image, 2009).

Christ as we speak the truth in love. I use the term *pathway* because Jesus declared He was the way, the truth, and the life. He gives us a directive, sets us free, and reveals His glory as we partner with Him. What dynamics are illustrated here? The Old Testament commanded us to do His commandments and live, but gave us neither feet nor hands. However, through a better covenant, His grace enables us to soar like eagles.

Where the Old Testament brought incredible encounters, the Spirit was limited because it only came upon men and women for the occasion. No better illustration can be found than with Samson, whom God raised up as a judge in Israel before the time of the kings. God gifted Samson with incredible strength, yet his vanity ultimately led to his downfall. Betrayed by Delilah, he was blinded by the Philistines and enslaved. The story tells that God restored Samson's strength to bring destruction on his enemies while he forfeited his own life (Judg. 13–16).

In the New Covenant, God's commands are His means of enabling us, as the glory of God is made manifest in mankind being fully alive in Christ Jesus. Before Jesus was crucified, He commanded His disciples to "heal the sick, cleanse the lepers, raise the dead, cast out demons. Freely you have received, freely give" (Matt. 10:8). Fast-forward to Acts 3:1–10, we read the account of Peter and John en route to the temple to pray. As they were about to enter the temple, they encountered a man who had been lame since birth, begging for alms. Peter tells the man to look up. Expecting a handout, the man stares at the two men. In a discerning moment, Peter declares, "Silver or gold, I got none. But hey, how about a new pair of legs instead of alms? Come on, give me your hand. Now, get up and try them out" (author's paraphrase).

CHAPTER 24

Jesus, Our Pattern and Path

Talk the talk and walk the walk.

—Anonymous

After emphasizing encounters initiated by God and engagement through response, we should examine how the Son of Man walked through these interwoven dynamics. The Gospels provide us with little information about Jesus's formative years. We are told how he astounded the Jewish elders at twelve with his wisdom and insight, but the story is paused until eighteen years later. By thirty years of age, Jesus was ready to engage in what had been termed the greatest story ever told. Some have said that 90 percent of success is showing up at the right time. Such is the case when the Spirit leads, as Jesus's remaining works give testimony.

Water baptism was the first act of Jesus's public debut (Mark 1:9–10). As such, the destined sacrificial Lamb of God engages in an act of righteousness that sets His course to redeem mankind and fulfill the prophetic plan set in place from the beginning of history. It was an event so significant that the heavens opened, the Spirit descended upon Him, and the Father of lights roared His approval with a sound that rocked the audience.

The encounter was followed by a series of calls and responses, which no one who has heard the story will ever forget. Jesus leaves the awestruck crowd and follows the Spirit's prompting into a desert without food or water, where He is wearied beyond our imagination. It is not recorded whether He knew how long His trial might last. In our current legal system, the judge will give a sentence, stating the length of intended incarceration. Even then, there is the hope of parole. At the limits of His physical endurance,

Jesus shows His resolve to draw upon the source of His true identity, the Word. Purposed by the Father, empowered by the Spirit, and spoken by the Son, it was a showdown of eternal consequence. God was putting humanity on trial through one man to authenticate the laws of heaven. A human was required to break the curse through His sacrificial death, fulfilling the law on our behalf.

We see the account explained in Hebrews 2:17–18: "In all things He had to be made like His brethren, that He might be a merciful and faithful High Priest in things pertaining to God, to make propitiation for the sins of the people. For in that He Himself has suffered, being tempted, He is able to aid those who are tempted." This is what missiologists call *contextualization*. So here we see Jesus being prepared for the mission set before Him, sent out into the wilderness in weakness but returning in power. What an encounter, what an engaging time. Sustained by His resolve, convinced of who He was, and employing the weapons of warfare, Jesus returns, ready to walk into His destiny.

What can we draw from the story of Jesus in the wilderness? We have been given a holy calling to abide in Christ and walk as He did. For one thing, encounter creates a need for dependency. From the failures of Adam and Eve, we can agree that reliance on the Tree of Knowledge, i.e., self-preservation, self-reliance, and self-justification, has left us destitute, deprived, and desperate. If someone is drowning, they are helpless without the intervention of another. No other passage in Scripture more precisely shows the dichotomy between self-reliance and Holy Spirit dependency than Romans 7:25: "He acted to set things right in this life of contradictions where I want to serve God with all my heart and mind, but am pulled by the influence of sin to do something totally different" (MSG).

Paul made this point very clear by comparing his old nature with the new nature he had obtained through Christ's death, burial, and resurrection. He used the phrase "wretched man" to describe his life apart from Christ (Rom. 7:24). Even though the law was given to point the way to righteousness, it did nothing to empower fallen man to keep the law. The law revealed that we were sold under sin and in need of God's intervention, a plan of redemption through the perfect sacrifice of His Son. Man, apart from the abiding life of Christ, was bound under the law of sin and death to repeat the endless cycle. But where sin had won the day, God's grace through Christ broke through and destroyed its power of imprisonment. After Paul reflected on his pre-salvation encounter, with great exultation, he proclaimed his present reality: "There is therefore now no condemnation to those who are in Christ Jesus, who do not walk according to the flesh, but according to the Spirit. For the law of the Spirit of life in Christ Jesus has made me free from the law of sin and death" (Rom. 8:1–2).

There is no more extraordinary encounter for each of us than the gift of salvation. Through the action of the Holy Spirit, God speaks to our hearts and makes the choice evident. When I became a Christian, my conscience was brought to the forefront in what many have termed a revelation. Something had overridden my private thoughts and cognitive awareness. I was notably aware of a presence that awaited my acknowledgment and response. I became determined to engage and trust my conviction that what was about to happen was the right thing to do. I was open to the possibility that Jesus was the answer, but decided He would have to make Himself known to me so I'd be beyond all doubt.

I remember watching black-and-white TV reruns of *The Lone Ranger* when I was a kid. The program would always start with Rossini's "William Tell Overture." Above the accompaniment came the resounding words, "And now, let us return to the days of yesteryear." I think it's beneficial to revisit our initial experience of salvation occasionally. Heaven drew me, and with only the slightest bit of faith, I had broken through a veil, my heart and mind bearing witness. I was immediately aware that a monumental issue had been settled in me. It was my first revelation, and I was pretty taken aback. My best comparative scenario is when Dorothy, in *The Wizard of Oz*, steps out of a black, white, and gray home and into the living color of Oz after her house crashes.

As with her, I instinctively knew I was no longer in Kansas. I was now born again into new, unfailing hope. God had brought the encounter, and I was now on board, ready to boldly go where I had not gone before. But most of all, I was engaged on a mission with the Captain of My Salvation, and the rest is history.

Salvation is not just putting away the "filth of the flesh," but also having "the answer of a good conscience toward God" (1 Pet. 3:21). By baptism into Christ, God has shone His glory into our hearts. Unfortunately, there is much emphasis on our past, a place that Jesus seldom takes us. Jesus is present and future. Simply put, we don't encounter our past to engage our future; we engage when the Spirit draws us into the present moment to look to what the Father is saying and what He wants us to do. How, then, should we live? Is it following the way we walked as children of disobedience? God forbid! Having been called to walk as lights in a dark and perverse world, we must be resolute in our dependency, trusting in Him with all our determination and leaning not on our unilluminated perceptions, preconceived notions, and imaginations. It is a simple axiom, brothers and sisters: live by the Tree of Life.

Whenever we encounter two pathways in the wilderness, it is for us to choose the correct path, for where we should walk is well-marked in our hearts and will make all the difference.

I think it is good, from time to time, to rehearse our initial salvation experience.

Herein lies our hope and assurance, as the psalmist said: "I will walk at liberty, For I seek Your precepts" (Ps. 119:45). In a biblical context, *precepts* are commands for regulating moral conduct and maintaining right standing. Jesus never experienced moral failure. However, He still had to pay the cost of obedience. "Though He was a Son, *yet* He learned obedience by the things which He suffered. And having been perfected, He became the author of eternal salvation to all who obey Him" (Heb. 5:8–9). How often do we forget that, although He is our divine partner who brings us to the Father, He has been given all authority and grants us passage into life?

We see the working out of God's plans for our lives being intruded upon by the one who seeks to distract, hinder, and deter us from being effective saints in God's army. As the prophet Jonah cried at the end of his deep-sea dilemma, the lesson here should be, "Salvation is of the Lord" (Jonah 2:9). Only in Christ Jesus do we have both truth and grace. He is the beginning and the end of our salvation and everything in between. In all things, we are directed to come to Him, confident that what He asks of us is connected to what He has for us and who He wishes to be to us—a loving Father. This, again, is what the encounter/engagement dynamic is about: to continue bringing us gain-of-function as we grow in knowledge and power for His glory.

I realize that the sequence of events echoes the theme of my message: God speaks, we hear, we believe, we choose, and we take action. It is the essential *modus operandi* of the Spirit's ongoing and progressive role in our lives. The operational dynamic of the Spirit and God's Word is best summed up by Paul, who proclaims the gospel as the power that moves us "from faith to faith" (Rom. 1:17). Combined with beholding the glory of the Lord, we are transformed from glory to glory. For as many as received Him, He empowered them and gave them the right to become sons of God (John 1:12).

In our devotion to God, we must realize that His presence, His loving embrace, and His care are meant to transform us into the full image and power of His risen Son. Let us welcome encounters and not neglect a divine opportunity to know and serve a God continually devoted to our salvation. Let not the enemy drive a wedge between God's approach and the outcome of our engagement. Paul eloquently says, "Therefore, my brethren, you also have become dead to the law through the body of Christ, that you may be married to another—to Him who was raised from the dead, that we should bear fruit to God" (Rom. 7:4).

CHAPTER 25

TAKING IT TO THE STREETS

> We have renounced the hidden things of shame, ... by manifestation of the truth commending ourselves to every man's conscience in the sight of God. 3 But even if our gospel is veiled, it is veiled to those who are perishing.
>
> —2 Corinthians 4:2–3

The open heart, willing to do God's bidding, can do the impossible. The spiritually prosperous are those who are eager to bring their circumstances to the Lord, ask for His guidance, and trust that He will, as a loving Father, direct their paths and empower them to do His will. The beatitudes provide promises that require a prerequisite desire for God's blessing. "Blessed [spiritually prosperous] are those who hunger and thirst for righteousness, for they will be filled" (Matt. 5:6 NIV, brackets added). Consider Mary's response when approached by the angel Gabriel. We see that her heart was open and willing to engage. When a spiritual encounter leads to engagement, we, in turn, encounter a new motivational dynamic, one that opens up to us the operational dimensions of knowing our Creator.

In 2 Corinthians 4:7, Paul spoke of having our treasure in earthen vessels. I would be remiss if I were to assign the encounter role as only the Holy Spirit speaking to our hearts through a corporate prophetic message or an angelic visitation bearing a message from above. We have been called to give an account for the hope in us through our testimony of what God has done for us. Revelation 19:10 declares, "The testimony of Jesus is the spirit of prophecy." Many of us were taught that sharing the gospel with the unsaved meant equipping ourselves with tracts and appropriate verses. Having emerged from the early charismatic renewal days, we were taught to use the "Romans Road." That was the primary tool for leading someone to Christ.

If memorizing a few Pauline verses and taking them to the streets was the solution for saving people, how then were multitudes added daily to the church when Saul (Paul) was not yet converted, let alone before he had written his epistle to the Roman church? Later, Paul went on to say that he was not ashamed of the gospel, for it is the power of God that brings salvation. What was it then that Paul possessed that convicted hearts, won over magistrates, and established churches on two continents?

To answer these questions, we first need a biblical perspective on "good news." After Christ's death and ascension, the early apostles and newly converted disciples did not yet have the New Testament Scriptures. Yet, many were saved by testimony and the teaching of doctrine received at the apostles' feet. In other words, it was oral testimony backed by the working of miracles, healing, and deliverance that broke through and impacted the multitudes.

What brought about such an explosion? As we read in Acts 2, following the outpouring of the Spirit in the upper room, something captured the hearers' attention and drew them to the 120 gathered at Pentecost. This is a critical observation that poses a key element in effective evangelism. It states that devout men from surrounding regions and other nations, including those from Europe, Asia, Cyrene in Egypt, and Libya, were present in Jerusalem then (Acts 2:8–11). How clever is the Spirit of God to take advantage of the Jewish celebration where many of the Hellenistic Jews had made the pilgrimage to attend a major festival? The upper room, therefore, must have been located near the temple when a heavenly wind and the following uproar began. Adding to the commotion was an unprecedented and unique event. Uncultured Galileans began declaring the extraordinary acts of God in the various languages spoken by the locals. Several words in Acts 2 describe their reactions as amazed, somewhat confused, astonished, and perplexed. In contemporary vernacular, we might refer to it as pandemonium.

The reaction, however, was mixed. Some wrote off the outburst, speculating that these Galilean hillbillies were three sheets to the wind. This was despite knowing that drunken men usually have difficulty speaking at all, let alone with proper articulation and accent. What a setup for the all-important question: What could this mean? Bingo! The heart that is open to the "what" rather than the "why" allows the hearer to receive and bear witness to the truth.

During a seminar on prophetic evangelism in Mechanicsburg, Pennsylvania, in 2003, prophet Graham Cooke presented two essential questions posed by the visiting representatives outside the upper room on the day of Pentecost. The first question posed by the onlookers in Acts 2:12 was, "What could all this mean?" The second question cut more profoundly to the heart. Those remaining said to Peter and the other apostles, "What shall we do?" (v. 37). To understand the context of these questions, Cooke explained that we often first seek to understand why a situation exists before we can trust and exercise our faith. The first question, "What's up?" created the space for Peter to bring prophetic history to bear on the moment.

> Peter's response was,
> "This is what was spoken by the prophet Joel:
> 'And it shall come to pass in the last days, says God,
> That I will pour out of My Spirit on all flesh;
> Your sons and your daughters shall prophesy,
> Your young men shall see visions,
> Your old men shall dream dreams.'"
>
> —Acts 2:16–17

God used supernatural means to break down intellectual and cultural barriers, reaching others of differing languages and customs. Jerusalem had become a hub for not only traditional Jewish converts but also Hellenistic Jews, who had immigrated from various regions to join the center of the newly found faith in Christ. We see in Acts 6:1 that "when the number of disciples was multiplying, a complaint arose against the Hebrews and the

Hellenists because the widows were being neglected in the daily distribution."

As the apostles gathered to resolve the present issue, we see the brilliance of the Holy Spirit (v. 2). The wisdom that emerged, in appointing seven men of good reputation to oversee the necessities of the saints, served not only to meet physical needs but also to bring together diverse cultures into agreement. There is power in agreement. Following this one act, in verse 6, it says, *"then the word of the Lord spread and disciples multiplied greatly."*

What occurs in Acts 6 has proven over time to be an established missiological principle, namely, contextualization. There is much to be said about understanding contextualization. It exemplifies God's wisdom when approaching other cultures, avoiding ethnocentrism, and sharing the gospel. The principle is well illustrated in 1 Corinthians 9:20–22, where Paul proclaims that he became all things to all men that he might by all means save some. In the next chapter, I will devote more time to utilizing supernatural gifts in evangelism.

CHAPTER 26

OUT OF THE SALTSHAKER

> Even if our gospel is [in some sense] hidden [behind a veil], it is hidden [only] to those who are perishing.
>
> —2 Corinthians 4:3 AMP

We are called to dispense the good news. Paul declares that the gospel contains power, resulting in salvation (Rom. 1:16). As ambassadors of the good news, we must recognize that power resides in words and actions. If we withhold ourselves and the witness of our faith from others, how can the good news have its intended effect? In this context, we bring an encounter and, with it, an anointing for change.

For this chapter, I borrowed the title of the book *Out of the Saltshaker*, written years ago by Rebecca Pippert.[15] I was intrigued to hear Ms. Pippert speak while attending the Urbana Missions Conference sponsored by InterVarsity Christian Fellowship/USA at the University of Illinois in 1987. Her powerful delivery and enthusiasm were so energizing that I was prompted to purchase her book. In it, she not only shares the struggles of overcoming the inertia and fears that we commonly face in evangelistic work, but she also exposes a tendency that much of the church has unfortunately adopted: a policy of avoidance. After reading the book, I set it aside for some time, only to revisit it years later as a book study for those interested in soul-winning and seeking advanced information. In addition to providing excellent guidelines, the book offers testimonials and encouragement to those primarily interested in joining evangelistic projects.

---

[15] Rebecca Pippert, *Out of the Saltshaker and into the World* (Downers Grove, IL: InterVarsity Press, 1987).

Salt is commonly dispensed from a shaker. The comparison is easily seen. We are, in fact, those who have heard and hosted the indwelling Spirit of God. The saltshaker analogy lends itself to the reference Jesus made when He proclaimed, "You are the salt of the earth" (Matt. 5:13). Most of us have heard teachings that describe salt as a means of preserving food from rotting or as essential for retaining bodily fluids in arid climates, let alone for enhancing the flavor of our daily consumables. The parable speaks of our intended influence in a fallen world characterized as hell-bent and in helpless deprivation. It was indeed the commissioning of the apostles and believers to be poured out as we spread the message of eternal salvation through Christ to the world. "It is the God who commanded light to shine out of darkness, who has shone in our hearts to give the light of the knowledge of the glory of God in the face of Jesus Christ. But we have this treasure in earthen vessels, that the excellence of the power may be of God and not of us" (2 Cor. 6–7).

As the saltshaker implies, salt is dispersed through openings at the top of the container. As believers, we are identified as being salt and light. Light has the effect of illumination and attracting attention to itself, while salt is meant to be poured out and flavor what it touches. Paul describes us as epistles, known and read by men. We are instructed to demonstrate and proclaim the power and love of an ever-present and relevant supernatural God through our actions and words. So, how do we demonstrate the goodness of God that leads to repentance and conversion? In other words, how do we bring the life-transforming encounter to the world around us?

At the same Urbana Missions Conference I attended at Urbana-Champaign, Illinois, in 1987, there was another keynote speaker named Ray Bakke, who has written several books on urban missiology. He made a statement that has never left my memory and has continually offered valuable insights regarding the Great Commission. He identified two major factors that explain why evangelicals fail to engage in soul-winning: "It is either for lack of information or motivation, or both."[16]

Simply put, motivation is the driving force that compels one to act. In a natural sense, whether by emotional response, for reasons of physical safety, or a thoughtful choice, actions engage the will to secure the desired outcome. Smelling freshly baked bread, securing one's seatbelt on takeoff, or volunteering to help a friend all involve our capacity to engage in decisions. Motivation is not exclusive to the natural mind, however. We, by the indwelling of the Spirit, have the mind of Christ, one that has a heavenly origin and is intentionally directed to each of us according to God's purpose: "For it is God who works in you, both to will and to work for his good pleasure" (Phil. 2:13 ESV).

The understanding is that there is another will at work desiring to reveal His good intentions while gaining our consent and partnership. Such a deal! He instills the desire and the motivation to carry out works that have been long anticipated, prescribed, and empowered. This is the source of our heavenly motivation, even the indwelling of the Spirit of God that constrained and compelled the disciples and church fathers to venture out into the surrounding regions of Jerusalem, Judea, and the world's uttermost parts. It was a compelling force for broadcasting the good news, performing signs and wonders, and making disciples in every nation.

> ... *two major contributing factors why evangelicals fail to engage in soul-winning. It is for either a lack of information or motivation, or both.*

Within the events recorded in the book of Acts, we see the operational and the effective pairing of the encounter/engagement

---

[16] Ray Bakke. "Taking Our Cities for God" sermon, Urbana Mission Conference. Champaine Ill. 1987

dynamic, empowering both with the authority (*exousia*) and the supernatural capability (*dunamis*). "And through the hands of the apostles many signs and wonders were done among the people" (Acts 5:12). If the apostles had chosen to remain in obscurity, they would have failed to advance a seemingly insignificant subcultural Jewish sect rather than into a worldwide movement. At this point, we should give credit to the Spirit of God. With the boldness of the indwelling Holy Spirit, the kingdom began to grow exponentially.

With the Spirit of God fully present today, let us consider some factors that limit involvement and success in soul-winning, at least in modern Western churches. Although the efforts of faith-based organizations have demonstrated compassion and philanthropy, there remains a minimal yield of practical conversions despite the time and effort invested. What is the essential element needed for both revival in the church and the increase of believers willing to accept Jesus as Lord and walk in the newness of life He offers? After seeing mixed results and experiencing fruitless attempts at soul-winning, we have retreated into the safety of our paneled walls, where comfort becomes the enemy of growth.

Where has the army been called to assemble, train, and be commissioned for combat? "[Jesus] said to them, 'The harvest truly *is* great, but the laborers *are* few; therefore pray the Lord of the harvest to send out laborers into His harvest'" (Matt. 9:38). There is much to be considered in the word "workers." Could it be that soul-winning implies work? While prayers move the hand of God, does He intend to go it alone when carrying out a mission? He has chosen us to co-labor with Him, to engage in the divine mission of soul-winning and discipleship here on earth.

Recall how in Luke 9:1–2, after Jesus had raised a little girl from the dead, it says, "When Jesus had called the Twelve together, he gave them power and authority to drive out all demons and to cure diseases, and he sent them out to proclaim the kingdom of God and to heal the sick" (NIV). Later, we witness Jesus, after multiplying fish and bread, having the disciples wait on those who had gathered. As finally recorded in Luke 10:1, Jesus now commissions an expanded detail of seventy- or seventy-two foot soldiers, equipped with *exousia* (authority) and *dunamis* (power), to spread the word and demonstrate its power by signs and wonders. Seventy or so were deployed under the direction and covering of their commanding officer, serving as a foretaste of things to come.

What do we see here: men not yet equipped with the Scriptures or the infilling of the Holy Spirit, marching in obedience alone? Having received salvation and power from on high, shouldn't we be better equipped for our appointed tasks in this hour? As a comforter, the Spirit dwells in us for our benefit; however, the anointing of the Spirit also comes upon us for the benefit of others.

Having pointed out the significant role of the Spirit as one who compels us to share the life of Christ, He is also the one who empowers us for service. Elaborating on the supernatural gifts given for the commission to which we are called, it is the impartation of faith that opens our hearts to hear and accept Christ into our hearts. And so, too, walking in Him is only possible through the supernatural empowerment of the Holy Spirit. We should conclude, therefore, as disciples, that we not only live by grace through faith but are enabled by faith to be witnesses of the gospel.

Our taking the gospel to the streets necessitates not only skill in approaching people going about their daily activities but also employing supernatural gifts, i.e., gifts that have been specifically developed and honed for the work at hand. The laboring Jesus calls us to will require preparation, dedication, and the strategic implementation necessary for such a task. Field studies, intel, data collection, and analysis are just some of the rigors that significantly affect the learning curve of a group's endeavors. Again, this may all sound somewhat regimented. However, there is a positive side. "There is joy in the presence of the angels of God over one sinner who repents" (Luke 15:10). It is a pre-given conclusion: the kingdom's advance is called to encounter tribulation, not labor alone. Consider that, by conventional strategy, any nation attempting to supply boots on the ground to protect its interests or advance behind enemy lines will require significant resources and skilled personnel.

The kingdom's advance in terms of acquisition and occupation will necessitate the employment of those who operate in the ascension gifts, namely apostles, prophets, evangelists, pastors, and teachers (Eph. 4:11). The primary function of those in this role is to equip and train individuals for ministry work. The laborers Jesus calls for are currently among us. Therefore, as a body of believers, we are called to pray to the Lord of the Harvest, not just for those who are foot soldiers, but also for the emergence of field commanders and the equipping of evangelists, prophets, and teachers. Some will have been involved and have experience in approach and delivery, while others will be interning during an in-the-field clinical observation and accountability period. For a further assessment of the operative dynamics, I've described a search through the Gospels, and the book of Acts models the methods Jesus and His disciples used to grow and build His church.

One might argue that Paul's apostolic mission primarily focused on preaching and teaching in the synagogues and appointing elders over the churches he established. We have several accounts from the book of Acts and the epistles where Paul raised spiritual offspring to carry on his work in the churches that arose through his various campaigns in Asia Minor, the Middle East, and Southern Europe. You can bet your bottom dollar that his generals and field commanders were well-schooled in the arts and skills of spiritual warfare and the operation of spiritual gifts. Should we of this present age be any less equipped and exercised for the exploits that have befallen us?

A great deal of emphasis has been placed on soul-winning books, programs, seminars, and conferences; the list is exhaustive and offers various approaches and strategies. It is only through partnership with the Holy Spirit that our hopes and efforts will yield fruit for God, for salvation is not in our hands to grant.

"Salvation belongs to the LORD" (Ps. 3:8). Only God has the power to save, regardless of circumstances or our efforts.

I want to offer a prayer at this moment.

Oh Lord, we beseech You—as a people you have called out and commissioned to preach the gospel with signs and wonders—that You call forth, raise, and release an evangelistic army having a complete and diverse range of supernatural capabilities, who are filled with a holy desire to advance Your kingdom on earth. Amen.

CHAPTER 27

Onward Christian Soldiers

No one should be safe from an encounter with the Holy Spirit.

—Bill Johnson

Christ's followers must be familiar with identifying the essential spiritual gifts for effective evangelism and giving examples of how they may be applied to the enterprise we undertake "as we go." Jesus instructed His disciples to pack lightly in terms of physical necessities. Since evangelism is a supernatural enterprise, we have been equipped with spiritual gifts, as listed in 1 Corinthians 12:8–10. As I was taught, these include gifts of understanding, gifts of declaration, and divine activity. All gifts are valuable; however, for the sake of expediency, I would like to highlight a few gifts that I consider essential for effective evangelism. They are, namely, discerning spirits, words of knowledge, and words of wisdom. These gifts are revelatory and require faith operating through love.

I believe the ministry of knowledge is the calling card that captivates attention and opens doors to further recognition and supernatural advancement. In other words, the ministry of knowledge creates space. We can see the operation of this gift in the account found in John 1:47–49:

> Jesus saw Nathanael coming toward Him, and said of him, "Behold, an Israelite indeed, in whom is no deceit!" Nathanael said to Him, "How do You know me?" Jesus answered and said to him, "Before Philip called you, when you were under the fig tree, I saw you." Nathanael answered and said to Him, "Rabbi, You are the Son of God! You are the King of Israel!"

One may understand that everything went well. Jesus, having made no declaration of who He was, uttered two words of knowledge—i.e., a character attribute and a reference to a previously undisclosed physical location—and that was all it took for Nathanael to receive eternal salvation. How often did Jesus use questions and simple statements to create space for a man's soul to reach out for revelation and resolution? This tactic is worthy of consideration, especially for those aspiring to effective evangelism.

Consider Jesus and the woman at the well (John 4:7–42). The disclosure of her marital status, a word of knowledge, rocked the Samaritan woman. Upon her return home and her testimony, a whole village was saved.

I particularly like how the heathen city of Nineveh was saved. God sends the prophet Jonah, the first evangelist mentioned in the Bible, to deliver a simple word: Repent. Attached is a word of wisdom that reveals a future action set to occur: "Forty more days and Nineveh will be overthrown" (Jonah 3:4). That's all it took, a simple encounter followed by an action that moved God's hand in sparing a ruthless nation.

Supernatural knowledge and wisdom, applied through revelation and prophetic words, can unlock the defenses or natural aversion that doubt may have. Hopefully, this helps us understand the verse that says, "Death and life are in the power of the tongue" (Prov. 18:21). The overarching point, however, is that power, in terms of authority or potential, is granted for restoring and building up the body of Christ. We become witnesses of God's redemptive work that is available to all who will open their hearts to a God who calls them to eternal life.

May we behold and embrace the hope of His calling and move in the power He bestowed upon us in Christ Jesus, so that we should shine as lights in dark and perverse times. Should we not accept His call as intercessors, agreeing with heaven, and as ambassadors, be willing to step into what the Spirit bids us?

CHAPTER 28

HEAVEN TO EARTH

> I will pour out my Spirit on all people. Your sons and daughters will prophesy, your old men will dream dreams, your young men will see visions.
>
> —Joel 2:28 NIV

Joel 2:28 offers an example of spiritual gifts in action, as demonstrated by the apostle Paul during his visit to Athens. In Acts 17, while awaiting the arrival of Silas and Timothy, Paul took the opportunity to survey the city, observe its people, and examine some of its religious customs in detail. It was not the hustle and bustle of the Athenians that troubled Paul. It was the fact that they were given to the worship of idols that provoked Paul's spirit within him. I'm sure all of us have been beset, saddened, and even angry when learning of fellow workers or neighbors who, after the death of a loved one, seek to consult a medium for comfort and hopefully encounter the dead. One only needs to listen to the nightly news to learn of wickedness in high places. We can feel righteous indignation rise when we hear of the inappropriate conduct of our elected officials and the homeland terrorism in our nation's cities.

Note the response to Paul's encounter when he addresses the Athenian citizens on Mars Hill in Acts 17, known as the Areopagus. In this forum, witnesses listened to the defense of accused murder suspects. After some spiritual reconnaissance, Paul makes his way to the scene for a debate. Did Paul go on a rant, reviling the philosophers and learned men gathered to hear someone they thought of as a babbler preaching about foreign gods? Nothing had transpired beyond Paul's reaction to what he had observed earlier. Paul was also an educated man who had recognized that his previous schooling and degrees as a Pharisee were worthless compared to the surpassing knowledge of Christ. An intellectual debate would be useless in engaging the Grecian intellectual crowd he was to confront. Curious, certain men ask a similar question to the one in Acts 2: "May we know what this new doctrine is of which you speak?" (Acts 17:19). This is followed by "We want to know what these things mean" (v. 20).

Paul rightly seized the moment by employing both supernatural knowledge and wisdom in his introduction and in developing the following rhetoric. Paul began,

> "Men of Athens, I perceive that in all things you are very religious; for as I was passing through and considering the objects of your worship, I even found an altar with this inscription:
> TO THE UNKNOWN GOD."
> —Acts 17:22–23

This account is further explored in the best-selling book *Eternity in Their Hearts* by Don Richardson.[17] He builds on a phrase from Ecclesiastes 3:11, "He has also set eternity in the human heart," which follows the belief that God has instilled in the human memory a capacity to know Him. The book deals with what is called by missiologists "redemptive analogies," i.e., things with a vague connection resembling some aspect or characteristic of a deity or transcendent power. Richardson discloses a fascinating story steeped in the Greek legend of a spiritual quest that occurred several centuries before, which tells of a plague that ravaged the countryside. In desperation, after seeking and sacrificing all known idols, the city council sought the help of an obscure oracle, Epimenides, to remedy the present curse. It was concluded that the plague would have continued even if all known deities had been sought and appeasements made. In desperation and by reason

---

[17] Don Richardson, *Eternity in Their Hearts* (Minneapolis: Bethany House Publishers, 2006).

alone, they concluded there may be a higher unknown power to reckon with.

Paul seized the moment and, taking advantage of their tradition, proclaimed the identity of the unknown god they worshiped. Continuing his monologue on Mars Hill, Paul declared that God sets all things and people in place with the hope that "they would seek him and perhaps reach out for him and find him, though he is not far from any one of us. 'For in him we live and move and have our being'" (Acts 17:27–28 NIV). The wisdom Paul employed reveals the brilliance of the Holy Spirit, as he explains, "As some of your own poets have said, 'We are his offspring'" (v. 28). It might be debated that Paul may have pulled this line out of context and repurposed it to clarify that the one true God is superior to all other gods. We have here in Paul's defense what came to be known as apologetics.

> For those seeking to gain ground in the art of encounter, the study of apologetics is recommended. Apologetics is defined as systematic argumentative discourse in defense of a doctrine. It is a discipline that involves a rational defense of the Christian Faith, deriving from the Greek word "apologia," which means "to defend" or "to make a defense." In essence, apologetics involves defending religious doctrines through systematic argumentation and discourse.[18]

You can readily see the analogy. Missionaries seeking to approach unreached people groups with the gospel will look for redemptive analogies in cultural artifacts, social and tribal customs, and history to draw parallels with the gospel message, thereby creating receptivity. Much has been written and evolved in the study of bringing encounters to the uttermost parts of the world. After all, we should continually endeavor to improve our methods and skills at reaching the lost. We would do well to consider the

---

[18] Anton Hein and Janet Hein, "Apologetics," *ApologeticsIndex.org*, accessed August 11, 2025, https://www.apologeticsindex.org/373-apologetics

admonition to "sanctify the Lord God in your hearts, and always be ready to give a defense to everyone who asks you a reason for the hope that is in you, with meekness and fear" (1 Pet. 3:15).

It is only through the sovereign grace of God that moves upon mortal man that the unbeliever can be willing to make the ultimate choice, acknowledging Jesus as Lord, repenting of their former ways, and accepting Christ into their heart. It is a supernatural endeavor of the Holy Spirit from beginning to end. Ultimately, it is God who makes us accepted in Christ Jesus. As such, He has chosen the foolish things of the world to confound the best of mankind's intentions and, in so doing, has called upon us to partner with Him in the grand quest of bringing many sons and daughters to glory through the sacrificial work of His Son.

CHAPTER 29

Encounter: My Time Had Come

Growing up in the 1960s was, in a word, a trip. It was a time when my generation was groping for meaning amidst military conflict, political corruption, and the pervasive fear that our society was on the "Eve of Destruction," as portrayed in Barry McGuire's song. Looking back now, I see it was a time of spiritual hunger, a quest for many, and I was near the head of the pack. The music of that time was inundated with alarms, warnings, and hopeful solutions. Eastern philosophy had gained entry through an emerging drug culture. Rock groups competed to spread a redeeming word to the disenfranchised. Many arose promising a "stairway to heaven," chanting mantras, assuming a lotus position, while listening to Indian ragas in rooms filled with cheap incense.

In writing this chapter, I was reminded of song lyrics that provided a background to my journey to Christ. As a hopeless romantic, I was drawn to the popular English band The Moody Blues during my college years. Somehow, the songwriters had read my mail out loud. With their poetic lyrics, soft harmonies, and profound personal appeal, I was captivated by their recurring message, which resonated with me. I became convinced that a transcendent encounter would somehow fulfill what I was desperately searching for—a divine connection.

The group sang of a familiar stranger who knew us and desired friendship. Who was the familiar stranger they sang of, the one who seemed to be calling? He referred to himself as our first love, the one who gives comfort and a sense of identity. I was now at an age when I realized that people, including myself, needed transcendent power, a higher power that seemed to elude me. Unfortunately, lofty dreams don't stay the course and secure a sense of spiritual assurance.

Encounter God and Engage

> *The Creator Himself intentionally left markers within the DNA of man, bearing witness to His nature and intention for us to be joined.*

Praise God. He found me on the first day of spring in 1973, during what is now known as the Jesus Movement, and a dramatic new chapter in my life began. The issue of eternal salvation and meeting the God of the Bible had happened. As the seasons progressed, I continued to seek career and ministry involvement, but I remained unsettled, even after getting married and having our first child. Hoping to offer fatherly advice and guidance, a seasoned elder gave me an assignment. He wanted me to write down the history of my turbulent high school years up to my late twenties. I'll never forget as he read through my testimony and the events leading up to my conversion. "Boy, O'Riley, were you ever set up by the Holy Spirit, a total sucker for Christ." He sure got that right.

Just as "the heavens declare the glory of God" (Ps. 19:1), the Creator Himself intentionally left markers within man's DNA, bearing witness to His nature and intention for us to be joined. "For the grace of God that brings salvation has appeared to all men" (Titus 2:11).

The purpose of sharing this pilgrim's progress was to illustrate how looking over someone's shoulder shows how the Spirit moves through personal intervention to bring us into a personal relationship with the one true God. If we pray, listen, and are attentive, we gain valuable insight into engaging seekers in soul-convincing conversation. When we listen with the heart, not just the intellect, we partner with the Holy Spirit as He sets the stage for conversion. Although put into simple terms, evangelism recognizes what heaven has been working on in another's life. Having the mind of Christ, we can ask God for wisdom on how to step into the momentum He is already at work in. In my next chapter, I reveal more specifics and share some ideas from the experiences my wife and I have had with encounters sharing the gospel.

CHAPTER 30

CLOSE ENCOUNTERS OF THE THIRD KIND

> When she has found it, she calls her friends and neighbors together, saying, "Rejoice with me, for I have found the piece which I lost."
>
> —Luke 15:9

This encounter is what I term *the third kind of encounter*. When we bring a God encounter to someone who then engages, there is a fantastic sense of God's Spirit partnering with us. We gain a new understanding of how He desires to use us to reach one another.

We had just purchased a hot tub. The soft-sided, round type can be emptied and rolled to different locations for use in winter or summer. Our delivery had been delayed until early evening when a truck pulled up at the end of our driveway. Meanwhile, my wife was upstairs dressing for our night out. I went out to meet the deliveryman at the truck. The young man began apologizing for being late. He explained that two other employees had recently quit the local swimming pool and leisure company to pursue more favorable job opportunities, leaving the company understaffed.

As he began rolling the covered tub across my lawn, I mentioned a friend who, years before, had gone to work for a competitor of his company. After a few years, the person I mentioned was promoted to manager and later allowed to purchase a stake in the company's partnership. The deliveryman—let's call him Gus—responded that the idea sounded good and that he was considering a career change. I don't recall whether something in his voice resonated with my past career challenges, or if the Spirit prompted the next thought, or perhaps both. In that instant, I found myself saying something that turned the situation into a God encounter. I said, "Something tells me that it's not just a job change you're considering, but a necessary time of self-assessment, one of life's essential crossroads." Gus stopped abruptly, let go of the hot tub, pulled off his sunglasses, and said, "Wow, how can you know that?" I now realize God had set up a divine encounter with this guy. I had been selected and now elected as an emissary from on high. It was time to step up and deliver.

Jesus, when sending out the seventy, instructed them to take no thought for what they should say; the words would be put in their mouths as to what to say (Matt. 10:19–20). The next thing I said might sound outlandish, but consider how the Spirit, using the things of the world, confounds the wise or, in this case, the utterly desperate. What I was compelled to say was something of King James English. However, it wasn't from the Bible, but a famous quote from William Shakespeare: "This above all: to thine own self be true."

Jumping up and down, Gus pulled something that looked like a coin out of his pocket. His voice was breaking up as he admitted he was an alcoholic, currently undergoing therapy and outpatient treatment. Holding up the coin, Gus shouted that he had just completed two weeks of sobriety through Alcoholics Anonymous and was given a token of achievement which read, "And this above all: to thine own self be true." He was stunned. Meanwhile, my wife, who was listening to the entire encounter from inside our house, joined us. She immediately told Gus that the higher power AA calls on in its twelve steps to sobriety was none other than Jesus Christ Himself. In this situation, the higher power was the Spirit of God, who had heard Gus and was making Himself known.

As Gus stood there, astonished, my wife walked up to him and said, "Jesus is the only one with the power to deliver you and give you the confidence you need to move forward into a better place in your life now." Gus retorted, "So what do I have to do to accept Jesus?" As he quickly knelt, with his elbows on the edge of the hot tub, she led him in a prayer of repentance and salvation on the spot. We continued to denounce and break off addictive strongholds while he wept. Then Gus abruptly said, "Wait, I have to call my wife, who is currently in a detox unit in a local hospital, and tell her what just happened and what she also needs to do." Meanwhile, my wife went off to get a book for Gus about how to get free and stay free through prayer and partnership with Jesus.

This testimony reveals how the encounter was staged and unfolded. I've been using the word "encounter" as it pertains to our active role in offering encouragement, counsel, prayer, or simply a kind word spoken in passing. Our acts of service become a means by which God puts us on like a glove, reaching out and extending His influence accordingly. When speaking the truth in love to believers, we are, as architects, building up the body of Christ. To those who are not yet believers, we are the ones who sow the seeds of salvation.

In retrospect, I had listened to Gus's desire to get up and move on to a better job. Like the man at the pool of Bethesda, he had been stuck at a point in his life with no clear direction. My simple responses, drawn from life experiences, let him know I had heard and understood his situation. It seemed that I had broken his security code and was entirely in tune with him. When sharing what came to mind in response to the Shakespeare quote, all defenses were down.

The Holy Spirit had set up this encounter. I had no idea that Gus had a coin in his pocket, let alone why a secular tidbit of literature would have such an impact. It's called a word of knowledge to those familiar with spiritual gifts. As I thought about it later, it was like when Jesus told the disciples to catch a fish, find a coin in its mouth, and pay some back taxes. When moving in the stream where God directs, He will provide what is needed, sometimes even without our awareness.

Besides a discerning heart, God had given my wife ears that could hear the grass grow. The Holy Spirit knew my wife was listening upstairs. She had already tuned into what was happening and jumped into the now-rushing stream. And so there she was, my tag team evangelist. Just as Peter offered Cornelius words at Joppa, saying he should be saved. Here's the kicker: Initially, we had planned to save the delivery charge and drive to the store to pick up the tub with my trailer. Due to a shortage of help, the tub hadn't been transported to the store when we arrived. The manager then called the warehouse and offered to have the tub delivered to us for free later.

The circumstances were odd, but the timing was precise. God had heard the prayers of a desperate couple seeking deliverance and salvation. God knew our address and our longtime desire to make His salvation known. Engaging Gus was straightforward, honest, and filled with God's presence. If we remain open and available to the Spirit, we will see the unimaginable occur. God can make all things work together for good, not only for those who believe but for those who earnestly seek Him.

CHAPTER 31

JAILBREAK

I wanted to share a unique encounter that demonstrates how the Spirit guides us in what to say in the moment. In this instance, it wasn't a one-to-one situation but involved me and a small group of young men. It is essential to understand that just because the Spirit may give us a spontaneous, unknown insight, it doesn't mean God won't have us recall an experience, Scripture, or testimony to fit the moment. Selectivity is often a form of creativity, and when the Spirit calls on our memory or sanctified imagination, it speaks more of His intelligence than ours. We should not claim the ability to manifest supernatural gifts as accolades of our skill and anointing alone, but rather the faithfulness and grace of Jesus operating within us.

To maintain anonymity, I won't disclose the identity of the following agency, dates, or individuals' names. As a science teacher, I had been assigned to work in a secure facility for juvenile offenders. These were young adolescents who, having been arrested, were detained until their court date, after which the judge determined their appropriate remand. Since they're under sixteen years of age, the state of New York requires juveniles to receive educational instruction while in such a provisional residence. As a residential detention center, there were fewer restrictions than at the county jail. Certain privileges could be earned for good behavior. Unlike public schools, where the separation of church and state is observed, counselors were allowed to share religious materials. The small library even lent Bibles to the residents. A Protestant chaplain and a Catholic priest regularly visited the facility to counsel inmates who sought their assistance.

Groups of four to eight residents, grouped according to their behavioral standings, would file in with a juvenile care worker to receive the day's lesson assignment. While writing the daily assignment on the board, the care worker asked me a question. It had gotten around the facility that I was a born-again believer capable of clearly sharing my faith. She told me the clients wanted to know my opinion on a matter they had been debating. "Mr. O'Riley, do you believe that someone who committed murder can ever get into heaven?"

The question felt like someone had just slapped me on the back of my head. It wasn't just the question or the situation, but like the angel striking Paul, asleep in the Philippian jail, I was taken off guard. Immediately upon this unique encounter, the following struck me: This is a state-funded school, not a church, but God, *you are in this*. In a flash, I silently confessed to myself, "Lord, you are asking me to break the rules here. Okay, you're on. Now empower me with what I should do and say next."

Selectivity is often a form of creativity, and when the Spirit calls on our memory or sanctified imagination, it speaks more of His intelligence than ours.

As I turned to the six students who were scrutinizing me intensely, the words came out. "Every one of you is scheduled to face the judge for your actions." Looking each one in the eye, I told them that on that day, however, they will have an advocate, a lawyer speaking in their defense. For those found guilty, a judge will hand down a decision with a penalty deemed suitable for the offense.

I then said, "Here's what you all should know about when we give an account for our lives before God one day. We have all committed offenses worthy of judgment, and the penalty is death. It is then that the lawyer steps in and promptly announces to the court, 'Although the plaintiff is guilty and the sentence is justified, the penalty has already been paid, Your Honor.' The judge replies, 'Who took the blame for this person and paid the price?' Jesus steps in and says, 'It was me, Your Honor. I took the blame for everyone, regardless of the offense. On the cross, I became the murderer, the rapist, the drug lord, and the thief. And having been found guilty, I paid the penalty with my own life.'" It is incredible how the Spirit connects you to the Word in such a moment. The realization that "He made Him who knew no sin *to be* sin for us, that we might become the righteousness of God in Him" (2 Cor. 5:21) gave me instantaneous grounds to make my assertion.

Some in the room looked astonished at what had just happened, but others still wore a look that said, "So what, what's that to me?" That's when compassion came over me. I looked over the small gathering and asked, "Why would Jesus do such a thing?" Not expecting an answer, I shared, "Because Jesus considered you worth it. It cost Him the greatest price anyone could give, their own life. So, where does this leave us?" I continued, "How can any one of us say no to such an offer? Jesus has paid the price of admission into heaven for all y'all. And now, He leaves the choice to accept His sacrifice up to you."

As I turned back to the blackboard, I could feel the supernatural adrenaline leaving, and my self-awareness took over, causing my heart rate to rise. Still a bit dazed, I walked out into the facility's cafeteria after the class ended. The Catholic priest was sitting and waiting for an appointment, or so it seemed. He looked at me and noticed my strange gaze. "Are you doing okay?" he asked. I told him what had happened in my last class, the question, and my response. He softly replied, "You see this black suit and white collar I normally wear? It usually gets me into places where I can talk to people. In most situations, however, I typically receive only religious responses. As for you, my friend, you've been placed in a situation that offers a much better opportunity to share the good news." I've never forgotten that encounter, and I've often wondered what eternal impact it may have had on those young men.

CHAPTER 32

SILVER AND GOLD

I have provided several examples of encounter/engage dynamic connection throughout this book, drawing from biblical accounts and personal experience. As we seek to share the gospel over time, our approaches and methods of evangelism continue to evolve. I chose the title of this chapter based on the literary association that silver represents the appreciation of people and things that have gone before. Gold is associated with the value of new things. After explaining the parables of the kingdom in Matthew 13, Jesus states that it is acceptable to regard both old and new treasures (Matt. 13:52).

Much of my early training for evangelistic work was structured around approaches, debate, and rhetoric. It does fit the encounter/engage approach, but it was based on prescribed methods and the use of rote monologue. We learned how to avoid objections and respond with pre-written responses. Listening to someone's deepest concerns or doubts was not a skill I had practiced; it felt like answering questions someone had not asked. The people we found who seemed open typically had some previous religious background and were more easily accessible.

Besides acquiring a fixed set of apologetics, friendship evangelism was also practiced. I always felt that I was an undercover agent and somewhat subversive in my motives; we called it soul-winning and were wary of who might be keeping score. Did I reach any? Yes. A truck driver delivered shoes to various stores on behalf of the company I worked for. I must have witnessed to the guy for at least three years. After moving across the state, I received a letter a few years later stating that he had accepted the Lord and had undergone a radical change.

As I've shared my experiences with evangelism, I'm sure you've noticed that most success was not accomplished through canned responses to spiritual inquiries or outdated platitudes for those in need. According to the *Oxford Dictionary*, a platitude is "a remark or statement, especially one with a moral content, that has been used so often as to be uninteresting or unthought-provoking." [19] Not to discredit these types of efforts; many have heard the call to repentance and come to believe. We've all seen signs carried by well-meaning proselytes reading, "If you died today, would you go to heaven?" Although it's an honest question, according to God's design and eternal purpose for humanity, Christ's death and resurrection were not intended to only increase the number of people in the afterlife. As a post-modern society, our world has undergone rapid and extensive changes. Similarly, the means and methods of approaching evangelism have continued evolving.

During the Jesus Movement (late 1960s to mid-1970s), many college campuses experienced a surge in students flocking to local churches. They came with long hair, bell-bottom jeans, and tie-dye shirts. The Spirit was pouring out on sons and daughters in a way that had not been seen since the revivals of the post-World War II and Latter Rain movements of the late 1940s. As with revivals and church movements, there are periods of growth and decline. The young grow older and settle in while the next generation leaves home to seek their own. In the meantime, various evangelistic campaigns emerge with new strategies and outreach efforts to attract new church members.

I use silver as a metaphor to illustrate witnessing through distributing tracks, making door-to-door cold calls, and displaying signs bearing John 3:16. In the 1970s, we were encouraged to memorize a series of Scriptures from the book of Romans, known as the "Romans Road," as a map to lead someone to Christ. The Billy Graham Evangelistic Association taught us to recite the

---

[19] "Platitude," *Oxford Learner's Dictionaries*, Oxford University Press, accessed August 11, 2025, https://www.oxfordlearnersdictionaries.com/definition/english/platitude

"Sinner's Prayer" by rote. Back then, it did result in conversions. What changed? As the decades passed, with diminishing returns on conventional strategies, many began re-evaluating their approach based on receptivity to the message.

The factors that influence an individual's or a community's openness to the gospel are subject to change. The social, cultural, economic, educational, political, and media/entertainment industries, being subject to the spirit of the age, namely lawlessness, are at odds with the advancement of God's kingdom. These arenas are what Lance Wallnau identifies as the "mountains of influence," which affect our everyday lives. Jesus tells of a day when "lawlessness will abound, the love of many will grow cold" (Matt. 24:12). The good news, however, is: "When the enemy comes in like a flood, The Spirit of the Lord will lift up a standard against him" (Isa. 59:19). "In this world you will have trouble. But take heart! I have overcome the world" (John 16:33 NIV).

So, where do we focus on reaching the lost in our contemporary Western culture? Although there are pockets of radical conversions within the global church, I became curious to learn about the methods that were gaining success here in the USA. What were the most effective means of approaching the people we encounter daily? At least, what skills seemed most likely to engage a stranger in meaningful conversation?

Some people seem to possess a demeanor and style that draws people to them. They are safety nets, having favorable dispositions and a listening ear; they are the comforters. Others, like me, are more overt, quick to speak, and offer rational explanations; we are the motivators. Most others fall along the spectrum somewhere in between. God uses all personality types.

We have been inundated and overloaded with models and methods that appeal to our thoughts and emotions. Depending on scripted formulas and novel approaches, humans quickly let things become outdated. Years of employing such tactics have yielded limited results for the effort and expense invested in evangelical and outreach initiatives. Extracting the best from conventional methods has shown that it is time for something new, unconventional, out-of-the-box, supernatural, and biblically sound to enter fresh veins of gold.

Having come into a saving knowledge during a time known as the Jesus Movement, we saw thousands of baby boomers from many diverse mainline denominations come to Christ. As a generation, we were ready for new and authentic experiences, especially within our church fellowships. Secular music, both live and recorded, had been a dynamic and cohesive force driving my generation to break old social norms, think independently, and develop new means of expression.

With the new social revolution came a different brand of doing church and worship. It is the young who are the adapters of culture. What effectively reached one generation doesn't always translate to the next. I am convinced that, as it unfolds in the church age, God plans for subsequent generations to have evolving spiritual faculties by design. They see differently, hear differently, and are unsatisfied with shallow lectures on behavioral rectitude. They're hungry for truth and willing to sacrifice. When I see young adults going forward for prayer in my church, I sense God's favor upon them for their faith in the belief that "all the promises of God in Him are Yes, and in Him Amen" (2 Cor. 1:20). Gold is what the young bring. May those who see it draw it out, for it is our inheritance and divine privilege.

Young people marry, have children, and pursue careers that take them far and wide. Churches change as new leaders are called to start new fellowships. During the youth revival in the late 1960s, another movement emerged within contemporary churches: the "Charismatic Renewal." The renewal had grown out of the Pentecostal movement, having originated in the Azusa Street Revival at the turn of the 20th century. Many movements—led by preachers such as Aimee Semple McPherson and Kathryn Kuhlman—followed, marked by signs, wonders, and healings. By the mid-1970s, the topic of baptism in the Holy Spirit had become so prevalent that even the Catholic Church began to acknowledge spiritual gifts through the agency of David du Plessis, also known as "Mr. Pentecost."

Despite the eventual acceptance of spiritual gifts by many churches, the public operation of spiritual gifts began to wane during the 1980s and beyond, perhaps due to concerns about maintaining order, avoiding confusion among visitors, or the occurrence of awkward words that lacked a redemptive nature. To a great extent, corporate prophetic words have been set aside and relegated to small, private meetings attended by those familiar with their occurrence. When the supernatural, however, has no place in evangelism, unsaved people have no reference point for what God wants to say to them individually. In years past, the organ of receptivity was generally the ear, as attested by responses at large crusades. People who had grown up with some level of church involvement had at least heard the gospel message and could be renewed in their faith. That era in the USA has come and gone for the most part. Despite declining church attendance over the past few decades, a new movement of the Spirit has emerged. As contemporary prophetic ministry continues to evolve, the organ of receptivity has become the eye—people want to see, in their minds and hearts, how God sees them, and His desire for their spiritual fulfillment.

Some years back, I had a word spoken over me, and I was told that my prophetic gift would expand into prophetic evangelism. I wasn't sure how that would take form. Should I go alone or make connections with those who have had similar experiences? I decided to research the people in the field whose experience and training I might learn from. I went home that night, got online, and prayed, "Lord, I want to pursue the word I just received; direct me to a good source." The book that stood out was *Prophetic Evangelism* by Sean Smith,[20] a well-known speaker, author, and evangelist. Besides the Bible, it remained the only book I couldn't put down

---

[20] Sean Smith, *Prophetic Evangelism* (Shippensburg, PA: Destiny Image Publishers, 2004).

for some time. In his introduction, Sean shared the encounters and engagements he had experienced while conducting outreach evangelism on the University of California, Berkeley campus. He begins by describing the "cold turkey" approach, which employs a "from my mind to yours" method, akin to the Vulcan mind meld for Star Trek enthusiasts. Although it has some effect, it only brings with it *my* understanding, hoping to strike a chord in the hearer's mind.

Sean points out that Jesus never modeled such an approach with those who were unenlightened. We see that Jesus's encounters with the woman at the well, Philip's friend Nathanael, and Simon Peter at his boat did not focus on rhetoric. Intellectualism was only seen when exposing and confronting the hypocritical reasoning of the Pharisees. However, we don't see conversion following these instances. The exception may be in the case of Jesus's encounter with Nicodemus. Scholars vary on whether Nicodemus was born again and whether his eyes were opened to the kingdom. As we move forward, let's examine more closely three instances in which Jesus initiates an introductory encounter. We'll see how and what transpires as each person engages with the truth set before them, and Jesus's response to their faith in each situation.

CHAPTER 33

BACK ON YOUR FEET, OUT OF THE SHADE AND INTO THE HEAT

> Space, the final frontier.
> —Gene Roddenberry (*Star Trek* prologue)

No exegesis regarding the subject of encounter or engagement would be complete without examining the Master Himself. In the Gospels, Jesus models not just the heart of the Father's love, but He also demonstrates the ability to reach into the core of where people stood in their capacity to receive His words. He spoke to people's hearts in a way that left them a clear choice: to embrace the truth and walk in liberty or reject it. He always gave opportunities for free decisions that would lead to a deeper understanding of Himself. His calling of disciples, His conversation with Nicodemus, and His interaction with the women caught in adultery were all approached with mercy and respect.

What Jesus models for us is a specific and direct approach, one able to pierce the heart of those who are open to a supernatural encounter. His examples of encounters illustrate the significance of what His Word accomplishes. His words exposed the divide between the hearts and minds of those He spoke with. Remember that Jesus never said or did anything unless directed by His Father in heaven. After spending time in a heavenly encounter, He was ready and able to engage in the moment.

Let's examine the account of Philip and his friend Nathanael in John 1:43–51. Philip, who has met the Messiah spoken of by Moses and the prophets, invites Nathanael to come and see for himself. Was it for curiosity's sake or to disprove his friend's claim that Philip responded? We are not told, but it appears Philip knew his friend Nathanael well enough to be at least intrigued.

When engaging someone, hoping for a divine encounter, I can't say enough about qualifying your customer beforehand, if possible. A brief conversation can usually give me at least a sense of connecting with someone. Getting people to open up may not require a profound philosophical question. The best practice advice is to start with simple present-tense issues and see where it takes you. Philip had done his homework and was assisted with this conversation.

Upon approach, Nathanael's intent and notable character quickly came to Jesus's attention. Jesus greeted him as one deserving honor and respect. . . a good place to start. We only have one chance to make a first impression. "How do you know me?" quipped Nathanael. Nathanael's response here is key. Jesus's use of the word of knowledge was paramount. It was a calling card that was not easily dismissed. Nathanael's spirit receptor sites were now open. Jesus's reply, in essence, was, "Come on, I already checked you out. I had eyes on you all when you were chilling back in the shade, munching on a bagel." Excuse the slang; these men were Galilean hillbillies, as you recall, and Jesus, being the Word, had a good handle on effective communication with whomever He met. I'm sure He used the local vernacular without being patronizing.

As Sean Smith tells us in a YouTube interview with Josh Lewis, "Revelation from on high brings an atmosphere and space for the hearer and the Spirit to interact."[21] Years earlier, my wife shared a powerful experience with others after witnessing and praying with several workers at a local university campus deli. When led by the Spirit, we create a temporary relationship that becomes a platform for a *kairos* moment between two entities. Okay, back to Nathanael. Jesus then moved from the present and past, declaring future encounters headed Nathanael's way (v. 50). By now, Nathanael was wrecked for Jesus. His present and future

---

[21] Sean Smith. Interview with Josh Lewis. https://youtu.be/zH0iu3XrqHA?si=-UPCssl8zga_C9Bg 2019

were locked in as a disciple and eventually a world changer. Not all spiritual encounters may list specific future events; however, what is promised is a God-given future and hope in Christ (Jer. 29:11).

CHAPTER 34

I Heard It at the Drinking Fountain

Hearing something at the drinking fountain is commonly a metaphor for rumor and hearsay, but this was not so for one woman out fetching water at a well in the deserts of Samaria. Most are familiar with this encounter found in John 4:6–42, commonly referred to as the story of the woman at the well. Many sermons and songs have been preached and sung about destitution and redemption. Here is Jesus, taking the long way around to Galilee. Why? Perhaps it gave Him some downtime to ponder his next moves. It's not the first time He was led out into a desert, suffering from thirst, and experienced an encounter. This time, it was for a very different situation. Curiously, God will place us in a position of need, only to minister to someone lacking similar necessities out of our own need. In fact, to our natural reasoning, it appears coincidental, yet some events seem clandestine.

So, what shall we draw from this encounter? Isn't timing said to be everything? Not so fast. Context plays a significant role here. It's not just showing up with the goods like some peddler pushing widgets, but it needs to be at the right time and place. In spiritual terms, it's not just who has the Word, but the Word *and* the Spirit.

Time, place, and empowerment can mean the difference between a walk-off home run in the eleventh inning at Yankee Stadium or someone showing up for a professional job interview an hour late. It only follows that the best road to successful evangelism is the simultaneous convergence of all three components. So, how does that work? In answering this question, I recall Jesus speaking about the Holy Spirit in the Gospel of John, where He says, "However, when He, the Spirit of truth, has come, He will guide you into all truth" (16:13). And so, on Pentecost, those gathered received power from on high. The power and presence of the Holy Spirit, along with perfect timing, converged to manifest remarkably. The final requirement is our willingness to engage and work in tandem with the Holy Spirit. The same then holds in this hour. It is indeed a moment when the supernatural is colliding with the unredeemed, as so eloquently spoken of by highly recommended author Bill Johnson in the book *When Heaven Invades Earth*.[22]

Another vital component evident in the Samaritan woman's story is the concept of contextualization. It is the common ground where optimum social connections are made possible. Consider another reference to Jesus's ministry: "In all things He had to be made like *His* brethren, that He might be a merciful and faithful High Priest in things *pertaining* to God" (Heb. 2:17). This says it all: Emmanuel, God with us. We may not be called to disrobe and walk among the cannibals of Borneo to gain acceptance or some contrived idea of credibility. However, there have been excellent accounts of those called to tread where angels dare not go when preaching the gospel to indigenous peoples.

We do have opportunities to share while simply connecting with a waitress at a restaurant, starting a conversation at a laundry mat, or inviting a neighboring camper at a park over for s'mores. I have found that these simple scenarios, even if not for evangelism, serve as valuable practice. I've had several occasions where I've tested a word of knowledge that may not have led to mentioning Jesus. It allowed me to pray for the person afterward, sharpening my communication skills and honing my gift set. It's called *redeeming the time*.

At the well, Jesus set the stage by first addressing the water. By requesting her help, He established His humanity. She noted He was a Jew, and that a cultural barrier had been breached. Curious, she asked, "How is it that You, being a Jew, ask a drink from me,

---

[22] Bill Johnson, *When Heaven Invades Earth* (Shippensburg, PA: Destiny Image Publishers, 2016).

a Samaritan woman?" (John 4:9). Her curiosity now turned to intrigue as He turned her question around by saying, "If you knew the gift of God, and who it is who says to you, 'Give Me a drink,' you would have asked Him, and He would have given you living water" (v.10). She is confused. "Say what? Number one, how can you fetch water without a bucket? Do you think you got something on Jacob, who drank here?" (vv. 11–12, paraphrased). Jesus stayed the course by comparing natural water to spiritual water. By doing so, Jesus provided her with space to pursue the dialogue. She says, "Okay, give me some of this water you keep talking about" (v. 15, paraphrased). Her request had now moved into a spiritual inquiry. Jesus had led her right to where He could present a heavenly option, everlasting life.

Looking closely at the moment, Jesus presented truth as an invitation to experience eternal life for herself. However, it was a *kairos* moment—a personal word for her—Jesus decided, for her sake, to test her resolve further. He told her to fetch her husband and bring him there first (v.16). Alas, her story came out. "I'm not married." Here it comes—time for a word of knowledge. What he said next about her previous marriages conveyed a message that this man was a prophet with a direct line to heaven (v. 19). Realizing who she was speaking with, she expressed her desire to know and worship the Father. Jesus offered her hope by telling her God was also seeking worshippers and was about to turn the tables on current events. With her deepest desires now exposed, she sighed. "I know that Messiah is coming" (who is called Christ). "When He comes, He will tell us all things" (v. 25). Can't you see Him looking at her? There was a pause as their eyes met. "I who speak to you am He [the Messiah]" (v. 26). That was all it took. The disciples arrived, and she returned to town, sharing her encounter with everyone. So convincing was her testimony that an entire village was saved.

What chronologically follows should further strike at our hearts. As the disciples offered Jesus something to eat, He turned and spoke about a different type of food. It was doing the work of God and finishing the mission that sustained Him more than matzah and Manischewitz (a sweet kosher wine). Having been with Jesus for some time, given his odd response, they had stopped trying to figure out where He was going. Then, Jesus spoke about harvest cycles and declared that the wheat fields were ready for harvest. Notably, He commissioned them to spread the word and pray to the Lord of the Harvest to send out workers equipped for a Great Commission about to be launched. The message in this story is that, by prayerful examination, we can see both the divinity and humanity of Jesus wonderfully disclosed in the encounter.

CHAPTER 35

SOME TOOLS OF THE TRADE

Encounter is the catalyst that drives a movement. Engagement is what sustains it. Jesus said to Peter, "Let down your nets." As Peter heard and engaged, he stepped from a world bound by natural law into a transcendent spiritual dimension with no limitations and limitless power. After acquiescing to Jesus's suggestion, Peter, having retired from a night of futility, reluctantly agreed to let down his nets. Peter then underwent a mind-blowing event that set him adrift from the familiar shore. The scenario with Peter, the nets, and the abundance of fish became a metaphor for his future calling. It was a "nevertheless, but at thy word" encounter followed by a miraculous confirmation. It wasn't the only method Jesus would use to call His disciples. Sometimes, it was simply, "Follow me." The signs and wonders revealed His claim as the Messiah to those who followed Him.

We could draw similar observations from examples of how Peter, guided by the Spirit, brought about supernatural encounters by establishing the early church in Jerusalem and the surrounding regions of Judea. After Paul's unique encounter and conversion, he was commissioned to expand the apostolic work of Christianity, planting and developing churches and writing letters of encouragement, instruction, and warning. So impactful were the messages that Paul's epistles continue to serve as the foundation of our faith through the ages. The Acts of the Apostles have been recorded as a foundational source of our faith throughout history, and so is the relentless work of the Holy Spirit to guide and empower us on a journey that continues to unfold. It was indeed the operation of the supernatural that brought credibility to the gospel message. The actions and testimonies of healings, deliverance, and miracles gave validity to the reality of a risen Christ.

> *Encounter is the catalyst that drives a movement.*
> *Engagement is what sustains it.*

Further clarification is essential regarding the operation of supernatural gifts, as they are critical implements when paired with training and timing and serve as powerful assets in our pursuit of souls. It is vital to understand that only Jesus, as the Son of God, could minister without flaw. Prophecy does not interpret itself; the guidance of the Spirit is necessary (2 Peter 1:20, 21). "Beloved, do not believe every spirit, but test the spirits, whether they are of God" (1 John 4:1). Prophecy—being partial, progressive, and conditional—should meet the qualifications listed in 1 Corinthians 14:3, i.e., for comfort, edification, and exhortation. Public prophetic words are not for correction but rather should be redemptive.

As for corrective words, if knowledge of sin or error is revealed to someone, wisdom must be sought on how to approach the matter in a manner that aims at the repentance and empowerment of the person (Gal. 6:1). Danny Silk's book, *Culture of Honor*,[23] provides an outline for correction and restoration that surpasses any message I have ever heard or read regarding church discipline. Therefore, all who would speak as oracles and ambassadors for Christ should know that "the spirits of the prophets are subject to the prophets" (1 Cor. 14:32), and all are subject to the laws and liberties we have in Christ. "Let your conversation be always full of grace, seasoned with salt, so that you may know how to answer everyone" (Col. 4:6 NIV). Operating under the guidance of the Spirit, in line with Scripture, and accountable to reputable

---

[23] Danny Silk, *A Culture of Honor* (Shippensburg, PA: Destiny Image Publishers, 2013), 23.

authorities, the tools entrusted to us for blessing and building up one another in the faith help to fulfill the purpose of ministry, that we all come "to the measure of the stature of the fullness of Christ" (Eph. 4:13).

PART FIVE

MARCHING ORDERS

CHAPTER 36

DISCIPLING THE DISCIPLES

Who are His disciples? Those who keep His commandments. Correct, but who disciples the disciples? Jesus instructs His disciples to "Go therefore and make disciples of all the nations, baptizing them in the name of the Father and of the Son and of the Holy Spirit, teaching them to observe all things that I have commanded you" (Matt. 28:19–20). Making disciples, however, is a directive that has often been overlooked in our modern churches. Perhaps this is due to how churches measure success. Typically, regular attendance, offerings, social events, and engaging Sunday worship services become key indicators of spiritual wellness. When we stop at good activities and fill the pews, we forfeit a much higher calling and purpose for the church.

In the beginning, God commanded mankind to multiply and subdue the earth. His eternal purpose for man was to grow into the fullness of Christ. As a chosen race, God designed the human race to mature into a bride for His Son. In Rom. 7:4, Paul writes, "We are married to another, to Him who was raised from the dead, that we should bear fruit to God." Reproductivity is a function that defines all living organisms. From the beginning, God commanded that every creature multiply after its own kind (Gen. 1:22, 28). In other words, the evidence of a mature disciple is the capacity to make disciples.

Much has been written, and much can be said, about this component of the Great Commission. So, what instruction has been left to us regarding the reproduction of faithful followers? First off, the phrase "make disciples" has always thrown me off a bit. Making someone willing to follow a behavior regimen or code of conduct implies subjugation, with or without their consent. I remember my spiritual father's quote: "A man convinced against his will is of the same opinion still." Making someone want to do something, or changing their mind, must involve free choice. Altering an entire lifestyle without coercion doesn't align with the average human being's propensity for self-reliance and independence, especially in Western thought, which is rooted in the axioms of manifest destiny and self-determination.

The New Testament making of disciples necessitates that we study the model of the perfect disciple Himself. Jesus proclaims He is the way, the path, and the life (Rom. 14:6). Jesus is our example or pattern of how to walk the life we are called to follow. Being the pattern Son, how did He attain true discipleship? Who discipled Jesus? It says that "though He was a Son, yet He learned obedience *by the things which He suffered*" (Heb. 5:8, emphasis added). As the perfect Lamb of God, we can say that His suffering and all the hardships were situations that tested His patience, resolve, and trust, but most of all, faith in the Father who led Him through every choice and sustained Him through every temptation and trial. He persevered in the flesh, His soul being exceedingly sorrowful unto death. Despite the relentless attempts of the enemy to dissuade and distract Him from His mission, He endured for our benefit. No other man, born of a woman, could have stayed the course as He did, let alone endure the cross. So, where do we begin?

If a disciple must learn obedience, what are the steps and rules? What characterizations can we draw from Jesus's lifestyle that will cause us to emulate the one who sent Him? What personal dynamics were at play as He walked out His life? These are valid questions, all of which deserve our honest inquiry. Jesus was not only the model disciple, but also in Matthew 28:18–20, having been given all authority, He charges His disciples to go and make disciples. Did the disciples walk in the same perfect manner as Jesus? From all the accounts we read, they feared their boat would capsize with Jesus in it, sought to call down fire from heaven, and scattered at Jesus's arrest at Gethsemane.

Should we think they are much different today? This reasoning could tempt us to fall into a fatalistic trap. Apart from Christ, no good thing dwells in us. However, born of the Spirit, we have the perfect life of Christ living inside us. Let us not focus on our lack of faithfulness, but rather on His faithfulness, for even if our hearts condemn us, He is faithful. Walking out our faith is a matter of engagement and dependency on the one who abides in us and empowers us to carry out His will.

Here again, Jesus models leadership. His actions and words serve as a guide for us. After all, "He is the way, the truth, and the life" (John 14:6). It's been my observation that the efforts of church ministry to get the job done are through preaching or conducting Bible studies. Dear reader, it's not just a matter of productivity or doing the right stuff, but it requires reproductivity, replicating the lifestyle of those led by the Spirit in others, i.e., having the will and desire to seek the Father in devotion and demonstrating the love of God through their lives. It sounds like a tall order. Where do we begin? The four Gospels give us a definitive portrait of Jesus in His life on earth, and if we want to know what it means to be His disciple, the Gospels are likely where we start.

Walking out our faith is a matter of engagement and dependency on the one who abides in us and empowers us to carry out His will.

John's gospel shows us three complementary insights into what it means to follow Jesus, each demonstrated by Jesus Himself. In John's account of Jesus's dialogue with the Samaritan woman (John 4:7–39), we could say that a disciple of Jesus is a *worshipper, a servant, and a witness*. To follow Jesus, to be His disciple, doesn't mean church attendance, involvement, and the veneer of tolerance toward others we have odds with. It means, first and foremost, to worship the Father in spirit and truth (v. 23).

CHAPTER 37

GATHERING HIS WORSHIPPERS

In the introduction to this book, I outlined two venues regarding the encounter and engagement experience. The first involves the Holy Spirit's heavenly witness in our spirit. We encounter God's presence, by which we have the reassurance that we are His beloved children. Through encounter, God's Spirit awakens us to a heavenly relationship with His Son. His spirit gives us the capacity as sheep to hear His voice.

The second venue employs imparted faith with which we see, hear, and believe. As Paul declares in Gal. 2:20, "The life which I now live in the flesh I live by faith in the Son of God, who loved me and gave Himself for me." We are called to be co-laborers in Christ. Co-laboring is a partnership that requires us to actively embrace the leading of God's Spirit. It is engagement, therefore, that allows us to overcome, thrive, and display God's kingdom on earth as it is in heaven. No higher priority was placed upon our Lord's life and sacrifice. Jesus, whether alone or among His disciples, never departed from a sense of His Father's presence while embracing and engaging in doing the Father's will.

When we set about ignoring or disobeying the leading of the Lord, we are left to our own devices. Consequently, the enemy plays on our human frailties. In his book *The Kingdom of Self*, Earl Jabay dedicates an entire chapter to the infantile propensities inherent in every child. In the chapter entitled "His Majesty the Baby," Jabay describes how simple physical needs, such as hunger, diaper rash, and gas, were the starting points of self-centered concerns.[24] Sounds a bit cruel to make such insinuations for little

---

[24] Earl Jabay, "His Majesty the Baby," chap. 2 in *The Kingdom of Self* (Plainfield, NJ: Logos International, 1974), 7.

"baby boo." However, the harsh reality is that we are all born with a fallen nature and are prone to sin. "For all have sinned and fall short of the glory of God" (Rom. 3:23). Paul, in Romans 8, goes on to describe His pre-conversion dilemma:

> What I am doing, I do not understand. For what I will to do, that I do not practice; but what I hate, that I do. If, then, I do what I will not to do, I agree with the law that it is good. But now, it is no longer I who do it, but sin that dwells in me.
> —Rom. 7:15–17

Again, Paul speaks of our original sin nature and its entrapment under the law. Good news: "The law of the Spirit of life in Christ Jesus has made me free from the law of sin and death" (Rom. 8:2). Being subject, therefore, to a life that is sold under sin, none of us walks in the freedom that God has for us in Christ alone. Whether it's old habits, mindsets, or lies, we all tend to go with the flow of the world. Being subject to the enemy's wiles, we all come to Christ bearing the ill effects of the enemy seeking to rob, steal, and destroy. There is good news. In Christ, we have received forgiveness of sins and access to the indwelling Spirit. In Christ, we have been set free from the enemy's power and given access to God's grace, wherein we stand and are made ministers of a new and living covenant.

CHAPTER 38

SERVED OR SERVING?

As servants, Jesus calls us to wash one another's feet. It's one thing to show kindness and loyalty to those familiar and friendly. As mentioned earlier, Jesus is the pattern son—the prototype we are to exemplify here and now. "As He is, so are we in this world" (1 Jn. 4:17). Even in a secular context, amiability and professionalism are always recommended when greeting a customer. This can be a tall order, especially when someone shows disrespect or is confrontational. My wife models the best solution. She first forgives the offender, then prays that they are not a danger to themselves or others. Now that's admirable. My biggest challenge—having been a public school teacher throughout my professional career—is hearing the messages sent out by liberal advocates of critical race theory, "woke" idealism, and redefined standards of social equity. These idealists often fail to adhere to their axioms, even to their fellow pundits. Jesus did not fail to call out the religious hypocrites of the day. The difference was that He exposed their actions and heart attitudes while offering them salvation, one that He would ultimately pay for with His life.

Servitude, as demonstrated by Jesus, was always set within the context of establishing an example for His disciples. His actions often set a precedent as an opportunity to embrace a higher law, reveal the Father's heart, and foreshadow the mission His disciples would be commissioned to carry out. Often, He would use examples dictated in the law of Moses, such as, "You have heard that it was said [a]to those of old, 'You shall not commit adultery.' 28 But I say to you that whoever looks at a woman to lust for her has already committed adultery with her in his heart" (Matt. 5:27–28). By such, He moved the unattainable standard to a measure that only salvation could secure. It was a new standard, not based on blind obedience but partnership. It was the heart of man that Jesus came to redeem, not just the keeping of the law.

As said previously, the encounter is a Spirit-led moment in God's timing and initiative. Yes, we seek Him until He answers; however, He chooses when, what, and how. The encounter then challenges our faith. That's where we must exercise our faith and stand in what we have been led and chosen to believe. This is where convenience flies out the window, leaving us in a difficult spot. It's not the same as cruising to heaven. It may be a time of incredible encounters when the saints gather, the worship team has us charged up, or we stand, hands lifted, and wait in His presence with a sense of awe. Soon, the service will end, and we will say our goodbyes and drive home with a renewed hope that all is well. Then comes Monday, and yesterday's anointing seems to "vanish in the haze." The book of Acts is filled with significant events, heroic deeds, and miracles. Yes, but how often do we realize there were many Mondays between such events?

Jesus clearly stated, "This is the work of God, that you believe in Him whom He sent" (John 6:29). Our abundant life in Him will cost us at times, but that's where we're destined to head, from glory to glory. As Christians, what we need will be provided, but higher realms are made available to those who will persevere and stay the course. The most encouraging aspect of this is the partnership we experience and the knowledge not only of His presence, but also of His ways. I was taught early in my walk that our confidence is based on our understanding of Christ as He shares His heart with us along the way.

Out of this abundance of confidence, we stand ready to serve one another. Not just to uphold the convictions we seek to maintain, but, as the Word says, "Bear one another's burdens, and so fulfill the law of Christ" (Gal. 6:2). Jesus, speaking of the Holy Spirit, says, "When He, the Spirit of truth, has come, He will guide you into all truth" (John 16:13). "The Spirit Himself bears witness with our spirit that we are children of God" (Rom. 8:16). The Spirit is the helper that dwells in us for our own sake. However, we often experience the same Spirit coming upon us, empowering us for special services. The gifts of the Spirit are different ways available to build up, comfort, and exhort one another (1 Cor. 12:8–10).

CHAPTER 39

Not All That Glitters Is Gold

> The woman saw that the tree was good for food, that it was pleasant to the eyes, and a tree desirable to make one wise, she took of its fruit and ate.
>
> —Genesis 3:6

A more accurate translation of *desirable* is, "wanted or wished for as being an attractive, useful, or necessary course of action."[25] My sales training in earlier years taught me that to justify the cost of an item, it was essential to point out features and benefits. Most purchases in the home furnishing industry I worked in were made as a result of emotional appeal. This is not surprising, given the barrage of advertising we continually encounter, which aims to create a deficit and instill a perceived need for something we must have. In the case of Eve, it was intellectual capital and personal pride. The element of comparison between what I have and what I might further acquire was vividly displayed in the "garden incident." The devil had played identity politics and won.

A mounting concern arose as the enemy exploited Eve's limited capacity to discern the direction of his line of reasoning. Although she was created in God's image, the enemy was victorious in imposing duplicity, which led Eve to fall into it. Through craftiness and subtlety, the serpent was able to lure her to a solution that promised to resolve the apparent dilemma. The idea was attractive and seemed beneficial. She contemplated what lay before her, then picked and ate the fruit. Contemplation is the key word here. Not only was the fruit visually appealing, but

---

[25] "Desirable," *Oxford Learner's Dictionaries*, Oxford University Press, accessed August 11, 2025, https://www.oxfordlearnersdictionaries.com/definition/english/desirable.

it also became the subject of contemplation. Her undoing was her failure to follow God's instructions and allowing the enemy's deceptive logic to manipulate.

Paul writes, "I fear, lest somehow, as the serpent deceived Eve by his craftiness, so your minds may be corrupted from the simplicity that is in Christ" (2 Cor. 11:3). There was a reckoning that preceded action. This was a very fateful event involving an encounter and an act of the will. Somehow, the capacity to deceive and beguile, a characteristic of enemy tactics, was instantly passed on to Eve. She was now like God, having power and being accountable only to herself. Turning now to Adam, something very alluring knocked him off his game. "Come on in, the water's fine," was all it took. The enemy working in partnership with the human conscience is a powerful tool and forms the basis of witchcraft. In any event, giving somewhat less thought to the matter, Adam took the bait—hook, line, and sinker.

At this point, a world under the delegated authority given by God to Adam was abdicated to the enemy of our souls. Not the encounter but the choice—misguided by indifference and desire—changed history. And so, the pattern continues. Inferiority and insecurity become the landing strip for corruption and the degradation of humanity. If we look a bit closer, we see the underlying root of the enemy's ploy. More than the demise of mankind, the enemy expressed his total disdain for the One who subjected him to eternal judgment and banishment.

As undercover emissaries of hell, the devil sends his minions out to sow seeds of every vice under the sun to discredit and denigrate God's crown of creation, even His beloved children. Praise God that there was always an alternative plan for man's redemption in Christ Jesus. Rev. 13:8 speaks of "...the Lamb slain from the foundation of the world." The wording indicates that the Lamb, commonly understood to be Jesus, was, in the eternal perspective, sacrificed before the creation of the world. While His physical crucifixion happened in first-century Jerusalem, the plan for redemption existed in the eternal counsel of God even before time began.

Deception, to me, is one of the most prominent devices the enemy levies to confuse and detach us from our trust in and obedience to our loving Father. Jesus was adamant in warning us the devil "does not stand in the truth, because there is no truth in him. When he speaks a lie, he speaks from his *resources,* for he is a liar and the father of it" (John 8:44). Playing upon a fallen race's vulnerability and sinful nature provides the arena of our deception. It is the enemy's lies that have most corrupted the conscience of man regarding our image of who God is. The weapon the enemy forms against us is two-fold in this regard.

Earlier, I referred to the passage in Daniel 7:25, which exposes how the enemy seeks to weary us through lies and prevent our pure devotion to God's lordship. It is a battle for the human mind. To wear out and derail the saints of the Most High, he uses the same tactics seen in the garden. It is the net result of misguided and sinister reasoning that is weaponized against us. If the enemy can get us to doubt God's love, promises, and intentions for us, to whatever extent we have accepted his lies, it will result in fearful outcomes, disbelief, and sin. When we align our thinking with his encounter, it leads us to engage in unbelief, resulting in sin and separation. It is the subtle nature of the encounters the enemy brings, convincing us to engage through rational deduction, emotional uncertainty, and the presentation of plausible solutions that all lead to an apparent resolution. This is all followed by a temporary easement of anxiety, fear, or desire that advances the enemy's ill-fated plans for us. It pays to adhere to Paul's admonition to "put on the whole armor of God, that you may be able to stand against the wiles of the devil" (Eph. 6:11).

In my experience and research, all unhealthy obsession, compulsivity, dependency, and addiction are founded on lies and deception that come to steal, kill, and destroy our self-image. If we are created in God's image, it only makes sense, therefore, that the enemy of our souls would seek to supplant that image and replace it with his own. He plays upon that false image and reinforces the deceptive power to gain access to our will. The image, on many occasions, will present what may seem good, perfect, and acceptable. This is where it becomes critical that we are led by the Spirit and not lured by convincing arguments, convention, or concessions.

An all-too-revealing scenario unfolds in Matthew's Gospel when, after Jesus has bestowed the keys to the kingdom on Peter. Peter begins to advise Jesus of the calamity that His crucifixion would cause, especially to His reputation as the conquering Messiah. Recall that Jesus made Himself of no reputation. When it seemed that Jesus's public relations was threatened, Peter defaulted to the Tree of the Knowledge of Good and Evil to offer an apparent solution to the dilemma at hand. In an instant, Jesus discerned the stench of Satan's reasoning. Seeking to derail Jesus's ultimate destiny, the enemy presents an apple of deception. Jesus won't bite. Can't you imagine an old haggard demon, defeated and limping off to crawl under a rock?

In John 10:10, Jesus declares that "The thief does not come except to steal, and to kill, and to destroy." Loyal to his nature, the enemy constantly seeks opportunities to cause us to doubt God's faithfulness, goodness, and protection. Besides dissuading our trust in God, the devil tempts us to doubt who we are in Christ. The last word God speaks to Jesus before He is led out into the wilderness is that he is His beloved Son (Lk. 3:22). After forty days, the devil comes to test the Father's word, "If you are the son of God ..." (Lk. 4:3). The devil's strategy was to question the truth of Jesus's self-image. Of course, Jesus quotes the Word of God and sends the devil back into hiding.

Is it not our self-image that the enemy targets? So, what is the self-image we are to carry? Should it not be the image that God has ordained for us? If we are accepted in the beloved, then shouldn't we embrace the truth of who God sees us as? Are we not washed and cleansed by the blood and made perfect in His sight? I appreciate Bill Johnson's words in this regard. "We cannot afford to have any thoughts regarding ourselves that are not in the mind of God toward us."[26]

We must comprehend Paul's message in Ephesians 6:11–13 regarding the armor of God. While down and out in a cell, some have suggested that Paul wrote the metaphor as he observed a jailer dressed in Roman armor. He connects each piece of armor with the defensive attributes necessary to ward off the proverbial enemy's attacks. The waistband girdles our midsection, protecting the vital organs that digest and absorb the world's sustenance. The helmet protects our processing center, the most strategic faculty, and often a targeted area. Faith, however, is the lifeline to heaven that guides and anchors the soul and most wards off the enemy's onslaught.

An army is often depicted as boots on the ground. The boots provide sure footing and stabilization as we walk out on the uncertain ground and the slippery slopes life throws at us. We are called to be good soldiers and told that we are to endure hardship and therefore not entangle ourselves in the affairs and distractions of this life (2 Tim. 2:3–4). Being grounded in the Word is essential when combined with faith in carrying out marching orders while advancing the kingdom. The one weapon that gives an offensive advantage is the Word. Consider, as we were taught in our formative Christian years, that Jesus did not engage in conversation with the devil while in the wilderness but quoted Scripture. Jesus had to overcome the enemy's encounters with a more excellent encounter. Jesus was being prepared to engage in His public ministry through His testing. When the Bible describes Jesus as tempted in all points, as all humanity experiences, He fought the good fight using the sword assigned to Him, even the Word. No other tool excels in spiritual surgery and the battle for our minds as does the Word.

Further encouragement from Isaiah 54:17:

---

[26] Bill Johnson, quoted in "Bill Quotes," *AZQuotes*, accessed August 11, 2025, https://www.azquotes.com/quote/1316807.

> "No weapon formed against you shall prosper,
> And every tongue which rises against you in judgment
> You shall condemn.
> This is the heritage of the servants of the Lord,
> And their righteousness is from Me,"
> Says the Lord.
>
> —NKJV

When it is said that no weapon formed against you shall prosper, it is not referring to diseases, pestilences, pandemics, physical harm, or the lies and deceptions perpetrated by the enemy against us. What is at stake is our testimony of who God is and what He has accomplished through Christ for us, the redeemed. In Rev. 12:1, the Bible declares, "They overcame him (the enemy) by the blood of the Lamb and by the word of their testimony." It is our declaration of the truth that brings a verdict that both judges the enemy and puts him to flight. The very weapon he would use to defame and take us out of action will be weaponized against him. Praise God.

CHAPTER 40

WHEN ENCOUNTER BRINGS CONFLICT

... stand against the wiles of the devil. For we do not wrestle against flesh and blood.

—Ephesians 6:11–12

Too many of us fall short in our understanding of spiritual warfare. We learn to tolerate or even enable the persistence of things we ought not. Neglecting our salvation rather than working out our salvation with fear and all due diligence has left many Christians subject to a less-than-abundant life. When mom and/or dad don't provide a steadfast environment of Christian values and hope, their offspring may find themselves, despite being good taxpaying citizens, struggling in their marriages or living in discouragement amid life's challenges in trying times.

In the previous chapter, I introduced that not all encounters are sanctioned by the Holy Spirit. We encounter humans daily, whether in person or through the media. After all, we are social beings, and entertainment plays a significant role in our human discourse. Most of what we encounter is the sound of people going about their business, the hustle and bustle of information that connects us to others, and our responsibilities. However, some voices solicit responses based on personal values, political views, and socially popular beliefs.

It is at this juncture that the soul and "spirit of man" meet (see 1 Cor. 2:11). From this interface, we draw from our most profound convictions rather than habits and superficial preferences. Not all responses are superficial and may require a more rigorous response. Hebrews mentions a line of demarcation where the Word "penetrates even to dividing soul and spirit, joints and marrow; it judges the thoughts and attitudes of the heart" (Heb. 4:12 NIV). It is the very seat where our faith begins and secures our salvation.

Standing on God's Word and His promises to us is both a labor and a place of rest simultaneously. It is working to remain standing against doubts and silence at times. In teaching us about resting in Christ, prophet Graham Cooke tells us that rest is a weapon. "As we continue to rest in the Lord, we wear out the devil."[27] After the three temptations of Jesus in the wilderness, the enemy had had enough in the battle to derail Jesus just before the inauguration of His public ministry. However, in times of pressure and in the middle of trying situations, we are enlarged and advance in our faith more than at any other juncture. Paul says in Romans that he learned to glory in his tribulation, "knowing that tribulation produces perseverance; and perseverance, character; and character, hope. Now hope does not disappoint" (Rom. 5:3–5). You can take hope to the bank, figuratively speaking. The love leads us to toil but delivers us to higher understanding and empowerment in Christ. As God journeys from one glory to another, we often find hell in the hallway, where the voices that come to try our souls range from quiet nuance to raging clamor.

> *"As we continue to rest in the Lord,*
> *we wear out the devil."* —Graham Cooke

God has called us to be soldiers, not entangled with the affairs of this life. Neither are we to be as children, tossed by winds contrary to our endeavors. Many will pay significant amounts for gym memberships and private trainers to help them build their

---

[27] Graham Cooke, "Rest Is a Weapon," YouTube video, accessed August 11, 2025, https://www.youtube.com/watch?v=aGTRgDTrleA&list=RDaGTRgDTrleA&start_radio=1.

bodies. Paul's admonition offers a regimen fitting for those who take up the challenge and reach a level of spiritual fitness that produces lasting effects. He says in Hebrews 5:14 that "strong meat *belongs* to them that are of full age, even those who by reason of use have their senses exercised to discern both good and evil." There is no indication that we are to become callous or coldhearted in our dispositions; however, if we are to tread on the heights with feet like a deer, we need to develop a skill set that is only available as we partner with our heavenly Brother. Paul's highest regard for our Savior was to "know Him and the power of His resurrection, and the fellowship of His sufferings" (Phil. 3:10).

Finally, it is a day when we need to be as innocent as doves yet as wise as serpents. It is a combination that requires us to be tenderhearted, willing to show mercy, and quick to offer forgiveness. The analogy of a serpent might be misleading; however, consider that a snake is circumspect, i.e., it never closes its eyes to what is in its range of vision. A snake's tongue has sensors that monitor the slightest changes in the atmosphere, whether caused by movement or scent. The spiritual connection to this picture is scriptural and offers necessary guidance for navigating a world of clamor and competing voices. I shouldn't neglect to say that this admonition is only made possible by our union with Christ through faith, partnership, and supernatural enablement in the Spirit. But, "thanks be to God who always leads us in triumph in Christ" (2 Cor. 2:14).

CHAPTER 41

NO ONE IS AN ISLAND

Simon and Garfunkel released a song many years back called "I Am a Rock." The lyrics create a poetic image that may be all too familiar to many of us at various stages of life. The song is a satire that expresses the irony of a life marked by isolation, loneliness, and depression. One could only speculate on the contributing disappointments, trauma, abuse, and loss that led to the apparent message. If you are not familiar with the lyrics of this sad song and decide to look it up, don't fret. I promise to deliver a redemptive alternative, even some good news.

Talk about robbing, stealing, and destroying! Like the man at the pool of Bethesda in John 5, the subject of this story had become hopeless. He was in despair, finding himself isolated and subject to self-imposed solitary confinement. How one arrives in such a deplorable condition is the subject of many psychiatric publications and endless research on neurological disorders. The fact is that man—separated from God and subject to the consequences of sin—can only result in a doleful parody of God's intention for man fully alive in Christ. We are communal creatures by design: We are continually "being built together for a dwelling place of God in the Spirit" (Eph. 2:22). God's purpose in creating us in His image and likeness is to reflect His divine nature and serve together as a corporate expression, in its full glory, as a bride being prepared for the marriage feast of the Lamb.

Encounter is the invitation to engage with our brothers and sisters in Christ. God desires that we bless one another and express His glory in and through the church. We may have begun in a garden, but we will end up in a city. The ultimate endgame for the church age results in a New Jerusalem coming out of heaven, whose streets are lit by the Lamb who resides within the corporate community of the redeemed (Rev. 22:2, 5).

CHAPTER 42

AMBASSADORS OF THE WORD

> I am not ashamed of the gospel of Christ, for it is the power of God to salvation for everyone who believes.
>
> —Romans 1:16

Returning to my earlier discussion, the Spirit first initiates an encounter with God, which draws one to God's presence. From the moment we first become aware of God, the Spirit pursues us toward acknowledgment, faith, and confession. With our acceptance of Christ, we are born into a relationship that enables us to know Christ and the love of God. As babes, we desire the milk of the Word. From the Word, we are called to walk in a manner pleasing to the Lord and grow into Christ's fullness as mature saints.

Our spiritual eyes are opened when we are born again, and our hearts are awakened. Our spirits are immediately attuned to the voice of our Creator. "My sheep hear My voice, and I know them, and they follow Me. And I give them eternal life, and they shall never perish; neither shall anyone snatch them out of My hand" (John 10:27–28). Even in the natural world, when a lamb is born to a sheep, it is already familiar with its mother's call and knows where to locate its next feeding. So, either through circumstances or indirectly through others, God speaks and makes His wisdom available and evident.

Our God is a God who continually speaks to us. After all, that is why, in John, He's called the Word. Hearing the Scripture, "My sheep hear My voice" (John 10:27), I've always felt a sense of wonder over this passage. How can we hear His voice? He now resides in heaven, a spiritual realm beyond time and space. Yet somehow, we have been given receptors that facilitate encounters and provide grace for salvation. Titus puts it this way: "The grace of God that brings salvation has appeared to all men" (Titus 2:11). Is it not the glory of the Lord that overtakes the psalmist as he writes, "The heavens declare the glory of God; And the firmament shows His handiwork" (Ps. 19:1). My conviction is this: our ability to hear and speak is by design. Why else would a God who spoke creation into existence and sustains all things by the word of His power, not design us, according to His likeness, with the capacity to hear and speak?

The Word, however, not only feeds our souls and spirits, but also carries an urgency to speak out in response to the revelation the Word often brings. It's the indwelling Word in us that compels us to give expression and testimony of a living God. With the Word comes the power of God to bless, encourage, and heal. The revelation of Jesus gives us power to speak life to one another, for "the testimony of Jesus is the spirit of prophecy" (Rev. 19:10). Jesus said, "The words that I speak to you are spirit, and they are life" (John 6:63). The Word always seeks to fulfill its God-breathed purpose and not return void of effect. We read that it was said of the prophet Samuel, "Samuel grew, and the Lord was with him and *let none of his words fall to the ground*" (1 Sam. 3:19, emphasis added). The Lord is also with us; let us not withhold any good thing, including the Word He gives us to share. For such engagement of purpose, the Spirit eagerly awaits.

Bringing the Word to the believer or pre-believer will require those who will speak. We have all been called to go and preach; therefore, consider yourself sent. The word releases faith, and "comes by hearing, and hearing by the word of God" (Rom. 10:17). It is faith, by which man believes, and with his confession sets in motion God's power, even to the effecting of miracles and the moving of mountains. Walking in the Word is walking in both power and authority. Authority allows me to cast out demons and thwart the enemy's works. With our proclamation, the power of heaven is released not only to see God's hand move in the natural world but to "build yourselves up on your most holy faith, praying in the Holy Spirit" (Jude 1:20).

And so, with interpersonal relationships, encounters bring us into connections. Be a friend, be an advocate, be a neighbor. There will come a day when we will all give account for the actions done in this lifetime. Some will say they built Him a church, prophesied in His name, and made His name famous. It is so sad to look at all the time, effort, and resources spent, yet it's not what we did for Him and in His name, but what we did with Him, in loving partnership and obedience, that will bring everlasting fruit. And so, it comes back to "in him we live and move and have our being" (Acts 17:28).

The church is built on relationships and thrives on knowing Him, correctly discerning the body, and loving one another. As the Word says, "My sheep hear My voice" (John 10:27). It is indeed true that we "we should no longer be children, tossed to and fro and carried about with every wind of doctrine, by the trickery of men, in the cunning craftiness of deceitful plotting, but, speaking the truth in love, may grow up in all things into Him who is the head—Christ" (Eph. 4:15). God speaking through us to one another is the communion we have in Him. And so, we are built together into a dwelling place. What a glorious story. At times, it seems as though the unfolding plan God has destined in Christ verges on the edge of fantasy.

Encounters call us to step out. Encounters may reveal the truth; however, engagement is where experience is gained. Most of our waking experiences and responses are natural. When the water begins to boil over on the stove, it doesn't take divine intervention to decide whether the heat needs to be turned down. The natural response is what we're created with. It enables us to coexist in a world of stimulus and response. Along the way, we acquire various skills, whether it's driving a car, sewing, or swinging at a golf ball. Saying hello when someone says "good morning" requires no soul-searching reflection.

We employ our higher cognitive functions and spiritual faculties in making moral decisions, guided by the Holy Spirit, which cause us to grow in wisdom and knowledge. This process is, by its nature, supernatural. Encounter in this context is supernatural. The capacity to hear the voice of God is an imparted faculty that employs faith. Even faith that allows us to believe is imparted and empowered by the Spirit. The original King James Version reads: "The life which I now live in the flesh I live by faith of the Son of God, who loved me and gave Himself for me" (Gal. 2:20).

> *It's not what we did for Him and in His name, but what we did with Him, in loving partnership and obedience, that will bring everlasting fruit.*

It is indeed faith that connects us to the realities of heaven. We can hear, move, and live by faith according to His purpose. Faith releases its grace upon us, whether we are at the end of ourselves or stepping out into new territory. Faith is the currency of heaven. It holds all things together and moves us ahead in God's plans and purposes for his bride. We are a city built on a hill that lights the way, bringing hope and salvation to all mankind. It is where we encounter the atmosphere of His presence that renews and refreshes the soul, and where we find legacies worked out through our encounters.

The body of Christ is an unfolding mystery; however, it must be spiritually assessed. Although we know each other through recognition and familiarity, we see differently when we are born again. "If anyone is in Christ, he is a new creation; old things have passed away; behold, all things have become new" (2 Cor. 5:17). In all things, the body is a place of refuge and comfort, as well as a company of believers that actively advances the kingdom of God's rule and providence.

CHAPTER 43

REVIVED TO REVIVE: A BIT OF HISTORY

> Repent therefore and be converted, that your sins may be blotted out, so that times of refreshing may come from the presence of the Lord, and that He may send Jesus Christ, who was preached to you before, whom heaven must receive until the times of restoration of all things, which God has spoken by the mouth of all His holy prophets since the world began.
>
> —Acts 3:19–21

Some history would be fitting at this point. Revival in the New Testament dispensation is a compulsory event throughout the ages. The Lord's commissioning was to go into the world, spread the gospel, and make disciples. After Christianity's rapid growth during the Apostolic Age, the Roman church carried the message throughout much of Europe. Through false doctrines and political oppression, the church fell into an age of spiritual darkness. As the Roman Empire slowly disintegrated, monasticism began to appear throughout various sects of the Holy Roman Empire.

Monasticism, a religious lifestyle, was characterized by the renunciation of worldly pursuits to devote oneself fully to spiritual work. This practice became particularly influential in the early Middle Ages as monastic communities emerged, promoting Christianity, preserving knowledge, and shaping social structures in a post-Roman world. During the following centuries, the mandate given to Peter by Jesus, having been preserved in the cloisters of the faithful, began to take up Peter's mandate, to go to the ordinary people, and feed the Shepherd's sheep. As the foundation for a new move of the Spirit slowly permeated Europe, individuals began to sense the call to return to the simplicity of the gospel message.

At the close of the Middle Ages, Martin Luther posted the Ninety-Five Theses at Wittenberg, Germany, in 1517. The Protestant Reformation began with the revelation that salvation was not achieved through works or reserved for the privileged few, but through faith; whosoever believed could receive heavenly rebirth. From its humble onset, Europe experienced waves of revivals, culminating in the reshaping of feudalism, education, the arts, and the formation of various churches and missionary organizations. Various movements seeking religious freedom and those fleeing oppressive governments sailed to the Americas to live out their convictions and ideals.

The most graphic biblical illustration of revival occurs when Ezekiel, in an open vision, is shown a landfill containing the scattered remains of a once-active army (Ezekiel 37). The bones were evidence of a company of trained soldiers, designed to march in step, rally to the call of their commander, have their spears ready, and respond instantly. The regiment had employed weapons of warfare, subduing its adversaries, plundering their spoils, and occupying their territory. It is an intense encounter for Ezekiel. Still, he was taken by the Spirit and lowered into a massive pit of broken bones, thrust into an unpredictable situation he had not anticipated at all. We can infer from his orientation that the prophet was given a heavenly perspective, an observation from above. Undoubtedly, he never had a moment to ponder or ask why he was instructed to provide an account of what he witnessed. Indeed, this was an encounter of epic proportions. His engaging response was immediate and concise.

Although the valley of dry bones was not a historical event, there is much to learn in the vision about how our words can release either the hands of angels or the enemy's minions. Some things don't happen unless they're first spoken—a reminder that "death and life are in the power of the tongue" (Prov. 18:21).

Somehow, He who adjudicates over heaven and earth has set the rules of engagement that require earth-based operators to agree and partner with heaven's purpose. "Prophesy to these bones, and say to them, 'O dry bones, hear the word of the Lord! Thus says the Lord God to these bones: "Surely I will cause breath to enter into you, and you shall *live*"'" (Ezek. 37:4–5).

As I've said before, I love it when *Star Trek*'s Captain Jean-Luc Picard sets the coordinates for his next adventure and commands, "Engage." The Enterprise blasts off at warp speed in a dazzling light display to pursue its next mission. I can't help but use the overused cliché, "to boldly go where no one has gone before" in the *Star Trek* introduction. Such is the case with Ezekiel. The valley of the dry bones account, unique as it was, is not the final scene for revival.

> *Somehow, He who adjudicates over heaven and earth has set the rules of engagement that require earth-based operators to agree and partner with heaven's purpose.*

Fast-forward to the New Testament, where John the Baptist calls all to repent, receive forgiveness of sins, and prepare their hearts to engage the coming Messiah. A better covenant, waiting at the door, was about to break out. John, considered by Jesus to be the greatest of all prophets to date, was speaking of an encounter like no other in history, and with it, explicit actions for those who had ears to hear how to engage, confess their sins, receive God's forgiveness, and open the gates of their hearts to allow the King of glory to come in.

Though Christ had not yet paid the price for our sins, the call of John the Baptist spoke to Israel as a nation, God's chosen people. As Paul later proclaims, salvation was also intended for all people who have been under a curse resulting from one man's disobedience. For all have sinned and are dead in their trespasses. But God has set us free from the repeating cycle of sin and death through the obedience of one man, Jesus Christ. Having been redeemed by His blood, healed by His stripes, and empowered by His Spirit, we are now risen to the works God has prepared before time. The combined spoils of encounter and engagement produce one ready to serve and recruit others from the world's domain and bring them into the kingdom of our Lord. Daniel declares, "the people who know their God shall be strong, and carry out great exploits" (Dan. 11:32). This verse emphasizes that God's knowledge empowers those who stand firm in their beliefs, do not falter in the face of challenges, and remain steadfast in days of adversity.

CHAPTER 44

THE WEAVER AND THE WEB THAT HE MADE

> No one serving as a soldier gets entangled in civilian affairs, but rather tries to please his commanding officer.
>
> —2 Timothy 2:4 NIV

With Timothy, the challenge given by his mentor, Paul, was not to be distracted by temporal issues that would ultimately diminish his capacity to fulfill God's purpose and calling. The voices that draw us away, distract our cognitive awareness, and contend for our affections are ubiquitous, contagious, and demanding. Somehow, as a nation, with all our technology, we have ceded to the tyranny of the urgent, granting it the right to dictate our thoughts and actions. To a great extent, we have yielded to unseen forces that consume our emotional and mental faculties.

The voices we hear often contend with the simplicity of devotion Paul speaks of in 2 Corinthians 11: "I fear, lest somehow, as the serpent deceived Eve by his craftiness, so your minds may be corrupted from the simplicity that is in Christ" (v. 3). In C. S. Lewis's book *The Screwtape Letters*,[28] Wormwood says, "I will keep them busy", suggesting the enemy seeks to engage individuals in various concerns or pursuits to distract them from their faith. By yielding to priorities that rob our attention, we lose sight of the One who is continually yoked with us. The enemy's priority will always be to divert our attention away from Jesus and the power to overcome.

---

[28] C. S. Lewis, *The Screwtape Letters* (London: Geoffrey Bles) 1942

In his 1970 bestseller *Future Shock*,[29] author Alvin Toffler discusses the rapid advancement of technology, which threatens to reduce us to automatons, having mobilized us to live far below the potential we were designed for. To clarify, *future shock* refers to the physical and psychological strain experienced by individuals who struggle to adapt to the rapid pace of social and technological change.

Some years back, we hosted a prophetic worship weekend. The guest speaker, prophetess JoAnn McFatter, raised our awareness of the enemy's subtle plan to weary the saints and anesthetize our capacity to discern the still, small voice that guides us through murky waters and uncertain times. The Spirit expresses that there will be times when men's hearts will fail them for fear (Lk. 21:26). They will run to and fro, blindly seeking truth in a world of lies. Such people, lacking discernment, are easily led astray, manipulated, and mobilized by the forces of evil. Although not an alarmist, McFatter's warning served as a wake-up call that was not easily dismissed. How often calamity falls upon those who are content not to discern the times in which we live.

---

[29] Alvin Toffler, *Future Shock* (New York: Random House, 1970).

CHAPTER 45

THE BATTLE BELONGS TO THE LORD

There is a vast difference between a page and a knight; one has potential, the other has proven loyalty in battle. The kingdom is called to endure opposition and even violence (Matt. 11:12). "Everyone who wants to live a godly life in Christ Jesus will be persecuted" (2 Tim. 3:12 NIV). Our call to spiritual warfare may all seem to point to a militaristic predisposition concerning our devotion to a loving and gentle Savior. But, as previously mentioned, we're called to "be wise as serpents and harmless as doves" (Matt. 10:16). We can only live out the apparent contradictions set before us by abiding in Him.

Is a healthy church a "bride in combat boots?" Why bring up warfare? Jesus said about the end of the age, "you will hear of wars and rumors of wars" (Matt. 24:6). Wars are not limited to nation against nation. Still, wars are played out on the fronts of political conflict, racial bigotry, judicial tyranny, and gender confusion, to name a few. There is a vast battle for dominion over the hearts and minds of believers and non-believers alike. From record suicide rates among children to the drug cartels, sex trafficking industry, and the media with its barrage of diversity, equity, and inclusion (DEI) values, the hearts and minds of our next generations have been the target of destructive encounters that would thwart God's plan for His kingdom advance.

Fundamental Christianity 101 teaches us, "The thief comes only to steal and kill and destroy; I have come that they may have life, and have it to the full" (John 10:10). Here, the wording "steal, kill, destroy" describes the destructive intentions of the enemy as he launches his attacks against God and man, hoping to dispossess each of their mutual and eternal inheritance. Man's inhumanity to other humans throughout history should give credence to the fact that the devil and his devices have been at work and are presently alive and active here on earth. Fortunately, a special place in hell is designated as the devil's final destination. For those who may not know the devil's fate: "The devil, who deceived them, was cast into the lake of fire and brimstone where the beast and the false prophet are. And they will be tormented day and night forever and ever" (Rev. 20:10).

The Bible, however, has declared our ultimate victory and the enemy's overthrow. It is a hope forged in heaven, predetermined and made manifest by the Captain of Our Salvation, even the Hope of Glory Himself, Christ Jesus. In the meantime, we must hold our ground and fight the good fight of faith. It reminds me of a scene from the motion picture based on J. R. R. Tolkien's *The Lord of the Rings*,[30] when Gimli, the battle-tested dwarf, is about to engage the multitude of evil minions of Sauron at the gates of Mordor. In a hopeless battle of the ages, he raises his ax and declares, "outnumbered by the enemy, against all odds... what are we waiting for?"[31]

In the book of Joshua, we turn from epic fantasies and legends to actual, documented accounts of giants appearing in the land. Into enemy-occupied territory, a covert reconnaissance mission was dispatched over the Jordan. Hoping to gain critical enemy intelligence, the spies encountered a band of grotesque giants, whom the Israelites had not previously encountered throughout their extended sojourn. I'm unaware of any research that connects the giants Joshua, Caleb, and the other spies saw with those of the tribe of Gath.

It can only be speculated under what contributing environmental factors were present, or how far back the phenomenon of giantism within Goliath's genealogy may have gone. Perhaps these were the giants mobilized to ward off the advance of the Israeli invaders, a people delivered from Pharaoh

---

[30] J. R. R. Tolkien, *The Lord of the Rings* (London: George Allen & Unwin, 1954–55).
[31] Ibid.

by a vengeful, all-powerful God. After all, rumors and legends had been given a forty-year interval to develop into a very present threat of apocalyptic proportions for these ill-fated squatters. In any event, ten of the twelve Israelites returned, stricken with fear, and their self-image was reduced to the size of mere grasshoppers.

Speaking of fear, I refer again to Daniel 7:25, where the enemy seeks to persecute and weary the saints through lies, threats, and intimidation. Sounds like the same operative spirit as we consider the scenario with David and Goliath. It wasn't the formidable size of the Philistine that had petrified an entire army of proven warriors, but rather a litany of curses and threats levied at God's army that provided the sum of all fears to a terrified host. David, tested in the fire of various situations, was fearless that day and brought down the giant with his well-tested but primitive implement. "We who are alive *and* remain shall be caught up together with them in the clouds to meet the Lord in the air" (1 Thess. 4:17).

We now move on from the champions of faith who slew giants and, against all odds, conquered the enemies of God's chosen. From the early church and throughout the ages, history records many who were persecuted and martyred for their faith. Jesus said, "In the world you will have tribulation; but be of good cheer, I have overcome the world" (John 16:33). Therefore, the persecuted church must ask itself: Where do we stand today?

Not to get overly reactive or introspective, however, it is the tares the enemy sows that often arise to beset us. Who doesn't experience self-doubt, insecurity, and inferiority at times? Whether it is concerns for our health, well-being, or incompetence, our peace often seems to be at stake. These are the giants we all face that taunt us and leave us to think of ourselves as deficient. Were these not precisely the fears that Goliath posed to the hosts of Israel, which had immobilized them? So, where do we fix our attention? Hopefully not on the mental and emotional lies the enemy besets us with.

So, how should we then live? How do we combat and take our place as overcomers in this world? The question leads me back to the title of this chapter: "The Battle Belongs to the Lord." In her book *Taking on Goliath*,[32] author Barbara Yoder discusses a spirit of intimidation that instills fear and debilitation. Unable to break through demonic and intellectual ties that bind us, spiritual dysfunction and impotence ensue, rendering the soul powerless to advance. Taking on giants is not for the faint of heart. Even with the wisdom and counsel of Jesus, we hear the disciples groan in Luke 17 when faced with the formidable challenge of forgiving those who offend them, saying to the Lord, "Increase our faith" (v. 5)—a phrase translated to the vernacular as "oy vey" (a Yiddish expression of dismay or exasperation). One must step aside to kill giants and allow the Lord to slay the dragon. Despite all his conquests, David knew that some issues exceeded what he had learned before Goliath and on the battlefield. In his desperation, he would cry out, "When my heart is overwhelmed; Lead me to the rock that is higher than I" (Ps. 61:2). Sadly, we too often fail or give in when the battle gets hot, rather than exercising our faith, repenting, and granting the Holy Spirit access to our struggle.

Years back, a young pastor addressed a small group of men he was challenging. He mentioned that, when facing personal challenges, most men were often snared in what he termed a *credibility gap*. To illustrate, I once worked in a large hotel. As guys walked into the kitchen, the chef gave the usual greeting: "How's it going?" Each would respond with "doing all right." After about the fifth person, the chef would yell out, "So nobody's admitting anything, okay? Then let's get to work." Day after day, the comedy show would continue. In his book *Wild at Heart*, New York Times best-selling author John Eldredge devotes an entire chapter to the idea of "The Poser."[33] He describes how we have been indoctrinated by a Western macho illusion that men must portray a positive image, or at least when facing an internal struggle, always to maintain a stiff upper lip.

---

[32] Barbara Yoder, *Taking On the Goliath* (Lake Mary, FL: Charisma House, 2009).
[33] John Eldredge, *Wild at Heart* (Nashville: Thomas Nelson, 2001).

Why do we too often revert to similar self-imposed credibility standards? Jesus offered up "prayers and supplications, with vehement cries and tears to Him who was able to save Him from death" (Heb. 5:7). Acquainted with grief and sorrow, He learned obedience that elevated Him to His destiny. If a godly character, joy, and confidence are to be our lot, should we not follow in the same manner as He? Whether engaging in exploits or simply trusting Him, dependency is crucial to living in the kingdom. Putting on a fig leaf or a bearskin parka will never remedy our need.

A primary tactic the enemy uses to deter us from walking worthy of the calling we have been assigned in Christ is the impairment of our hearing. Given ears to hear in the Spirit, we possess a faculty enabling us to receive divine guidance. Failure to obey or disregard the still, small voice of God often leads to dullness that hinders this critical ability. In this way, the enemy works relentlessly on various levels to confuse and interrupt our spiritual receptors. With the intense distractions around us, we are constantly bombarded with random impulses. Ultimately, designed to sabotage our simple devotion, the intensity of many voices often overloads our neurological response apparatus with demands and competes for our attention. To put it bluntly, we are, for the most part, a culture stuck in a cycle of distraction and impulsiveness. Small wonder we have difficulty hearing heaven's still, small voice.

The other factor contributing to our impaired hearing is how we maintain the soil of our hearts. Jesus is the light of the world. As children of the light, we were designed to walk in the light of His counsel and leading. Without the consistent spiritual telemetry of heaven, we are left to configure our situations and operate on tenuous ground. With significantly less efficiency than needed to walk in grace effectively, we default to our natural habits and presuppositions. Action defaults to reaction; stepping aside from faith, we fall into unrest and unbelief. As unbelief and disobedience continue, our vision is blurred and our hearing capacity is impaired.

> *The encounter/engage dynamic is designed to guide, strengthen, and promote our maturity in Christ. It is where we hear, obey, and abide.*

It is often the little foxes that spoil the vineyard. Maintaining a heart that is open, soft, and teachable will usually require the discipline of taking short accounts and making mid-course corrections. A good test is what I call the peace meter. Philippians 4:6–7 says to "be anxious for nothing, but in everything by prayer and supplication, with thanksgiving, let your requests be made known to God; and the peace of God, which surpasses all understanding, will guard your hearts and minds through Christ Jesus." I once heard it said that peace is the umpire of our souls. Therefore, we should allow peace to govern our disposition and guide our discourse. Suffice it to say, it's not the peace the world offers or pursues, but by Christ abiding in us, we have a peace that passes understanding.

Encounter, besides embracing God's presence in the moment, is how the Spirit reaches out to us to comfort and assure us of the Father's love, His ever-vigilant attention, and His intervention on our behalf. The encounter/engage dynamic is a gateway that promotes our maturity in Christ.

Referring to John 15:16, we see the encounter and engagement dynamic clearly illustrated by Jesus Himself. "You did not choose Me, but I chose you and appointed you that you should go and bear fruit, and that your fruit should remain." We have been encouraged to come into His presence to adore Him, seek His counsel, and make petitions for others and ourselves. Now what? Fruit only happens as the Spirit directs, corrects, exhorts, and enlightens us to a superior perspective that necessitates obedience, commitment, and our willingness to engage. Knowing Christ is more than times of refreshment. According to Paul, it's death and resurrection. Jesus knew it. Now, it's our turn. We die daily, but fortunately, we are renewed daily. Some have called it the great exchange, where we offer our weakness and He, in turn, supplies His strength. Such a deal!

CHAPTER 46

LAST CALL

As explained at the beginning of this book, an encounter is described as a devotional experience where one yields their heart and attention to the presence of the Lord through prayer, praise, and worship. Our spirits join with the Holy Spirit, and we are lifted into heavenly realms where we are blessed, refreshed, and made one in His love. As Scripture tells us, "he who is joined to the Lord is one spirit with Him" (1 Corinthians 6:17). How often did Jesus draw away from the concerns of this life and pursue the loving presence of His Father in heaven? From His frequent encounters, Jesus moved in both power and authority through every aspect of His early ministry and administration. Similarly, we are called into communion within our devotional lives and as an assembly of believers, where we encounter the living God on a glorious corporate level.

While listening to a broadcast featuring Christine Caine one morning before work, I was impressed by an account of how easily we drift off course when we fail to maintain some healthy caution and spiritual markers. While merely spectating, we naturally tend to become critics. Christine described swimming with her sisters in the ocean along the Australian coast when she was young. Her father would set up large umbrellas as markers to prevent his daughters from drifting away from his watchful eyes.

It reminded me of a similar situation I had experienced. As a lifeguard working in a New York State Park along Lake Ontario, there were a few days when the waves were so significant that we would close the beach. Some of us more adventurous guards would head past the park boundaries to body surf and take advantage of the free moment. The prevailing winds in that region of the Great Lakes cause the waves to impact the shore at an angle, producing what are known as longshore currents. Without a reference point on the beach, within half an hour, we found we had shifted in undertow currents several hundred yards east of our towels and sweatshirts.

Here's the point. Without an anchor, our souls naturally tend to wander. There are just too many distractions competing for our attention. Jesus said, "In the world you will have tribulation; but be of good cheer, I have overcome the world" (John 16:33). Perhaps, knowing the condition of the fallen world, Jesus provided his admonishment while simultaneously offering the necessary navigational point of reference for those willing to swim upstream and fight the currents that face those determined to take on the challenges that spiritual maturing demands. Be assured that the risks are worth it. For those who require milk, your provisions will be brought to you. However, for those of uncommon faith, who are willing to endure the rigors of engagement and challenge, higher realms of knowing God's ways, His secrets, and the promise of more extraordinary encounters to come.

The key is resting in knowing our Savior's affections toward us and experiencing the presence of the Holy Spirit, through which we have full assurance of One whose sustaining grace is ever present to help us in times of need. Devotion and trust are the keys to the abundant life He came to lead us to. He is continually willing to show Himself strong on our behalf. Indeed, "in quietness and confidence shall be your strength" (Isa. 30:15). Even more so, His capacity extends beyond rescue, restoration, and deliverance from self-dependency and striving. May I emphasize that it is not constantly striving against poor judgment, bad habits, and unforgiveness? While not dismissing these common issues, it's the human effort we spend maintaining credibility—based on always trying to do what is right—that preoccupies and wears us out. Often, the suitable and seemingly appropriate measures we strive for will trip us up. Returning to the Word, the kingdom is not a matter of being right, but instead, "righteousness, peace and joy in the Holy Spirit" (Rom. 14:17 NIV). It is His abundant grace and love poured out upon us that grant us the opportunity to both encounter and engage Him in all His richness and glory.

As we conclude this narrative of the encounter and engagement dynamic, we realize that a much bigger picture is unfolding than simply walking out of daily routines and staying in our lanes, as it were. With increased vision, we're called to step out with those who pave the way for kingdom invasion. It's not for the fainthearted, but for those willing to make a difference with a heart, to be salt and light, rejoicing in hope and ever vigilant to the heavenly call. Salt is the divine seasoning and influence we bring to the world, bearing the light of God's knowledge and glory, which will draw those who seek salvation and fulfillment in their lives.

About the Author

Richard O'Riley is a retired public high school science teacher, college science instructor, and track and field coach. He has always been an advocate for public education and biblical equipping within the church, holding master's degrees in secondary education, science, and educational administration. Before teaching, Richard was elected as a parent representative and guest speaker at the National Economy and Education Convention, sponsored by the Rockefeller Foundation for Public Education.

For many years, he and Christine have served as elders in their church. He has written numerous brochures and articles, including blogs, on topics such as the empowerment of the Holy Spirit in the workplace and the operation of supernatural gifts in contemporary witnessing.

He and his wife, Christine, an RN, raised their six children in Rochester, New York, where he and Christine still live. Many of their children have gone on to pursue careers in government, teaching, business, healthcare administration, and the pharmaceutical industry. Now empty nesters, Richard and Christine enjoy hiking, writing, and traveling, along with hosting countless family gatherings.

Contact Richard:
Email: oriley6@aol.com
Facebook: www.facebook.com/dick.oriley

www.ingramcontent.com/pod-product-compliance
Lightning Source LLC
Chambersburg PA
CBHW060354080526
44583CB00012B/311